S. S Colt

The tourist's guide through the Empire state

Embracing all cities, towns and watering places, by Hudson river and New York

central route

S. S Colt

The tourist's guide through the Empire state
Embracing all cities, towns and watering places, by Hudson river and New York central route

ISBN/EAN: 9783744745796

Printed in Europe, USA, Canada, Australia, Japan

Cover: Foto ©Andreas Hilbeck / pixelio.de

More available books at **www.hansebooks.com**

THE

TOURIST'S GUIDE

THROUGH THE

EMPIRE STATE.

EMBRACING ALL

CITIES, TOWNS AND WATERING PLACES,

By Hudson River and New York Central Route.

DESCRIBING ALL ROUTES OF TRAVEL, AND PLACES OF POPULAR INTEREST AND RESORT ALONG THE HUDSON RIVER, LAKE GEORGE, LAKE CHAMPLAIN, THE ADIRONDACKS, SARATOGA, NIAGARA FALLS, ETC., ETC.

———•◆•———

Edited and Published by
MRS. S. S. COLT, ALBANY, N. Y.
1871.

1609.

HENDRICK HUDSON, and his Ship the Half-Moon.

This portrait of the bold navigator is copied from an Oil Painting, of undoubted authenticity, presented to the State by one of its oldest families, and now preserved in the City Hall, New York.

CONTENTS.

CHAPTER I.
A Birds-eye View of New York and its Environs .... PAGE 1

CHAPTER II.
New York to Irvington. Telling Old Stories and New Ones by the way 11

CHAPTER III.
From Irvington to West Point. Beecher's Home—Greeley's Farm 22

CHAPTER IV.
West Point to Albany. The West Point Cadets—the Beauties of Poughkeepsie, and the Story of *A Tongue that was Tamed!*.. 44

CHAPTER V.
Our Capital City. Its Sights and its People—Old Times and New! 71

CHAPTER VI.
Albany and Susquehanna Road. The Helderbergs—Howe's Cave—Sharon Springs—Richfield Springs—Cherry Valley 104

CHAPTER VII.

Cooperstown. The Home of Fenimore Cooper—Leatherstocking Falls—"Lake Glimmerglass" 122

CHAPTER VIII.

Troy—Ballston Spa—Saratoga and its Belles 134

CHAPTER IX.

Lake George—Lake Champlain—the Adirondacks—about Deer and Black Flies! 149

CHAPTER X.

Our Westward Way. Auburn—Cornell University—Taghkanic Falls—Rochester—Avon—Watkins Glen, etc 165

CHAPTER XI.

Buffalo and Niagara.................................... 188

CHAPTER XII.

Hints for Travelers..................................... 199

CHAPTER XIII.

Princess Nemona; or, Love in the Empire State 205

CHAPTER XIV.

Poem—Climbing up the Mountain......................... 213

CHAPTER XV.

Finis 220

𝔊ʟɪᴅɪɴɢ *viâ* steamboat,
    Riding *viâ* rail,—
Cicerone and Tourist,
    We unfold our tale.

𝔒ꜰꜰ from the beaten track
    We shall sometimes stray;
Sans weariness and care,
    Taking holiday!

𝔒ᴅᴅ places—legends queer—
    With those better known,
Will all be noted here,
    As we journey on!

𝔅ɪʀᴅs of every feather
    Travel now-a-days;
From grave and gay, together,
    We trust to merit praise!

𝔉ᴏʀ fun and fact *will* meet
    Viâ steamboat—*viâ* rail—
Where'er our Gᴜɪᴅᴇ, complete,
    Unfolds its pleasing tale!

THE TOURIST'S GUIDE.

THROUGH THE EMPIRE STATE lies our way. We shall sail up the legendary Hudson, renowned in the Old World and the New, noting its *Show Places*, and recounting its funny and pathetic stories of the present and the past.

The Hudson has a historic yesterday. Saratoga is society's Queen of to-day. From both we shall journey on to that sublime mountain-heart of New York, where the Satanic and beautiful Black Fly holds its revels, and the "panther's print lies fresh."

In the Adirondacks we shall find deer; pickerel in Lake Champlain; salmon in Lake George; and splendid scenery EVERYWHERE.

Our pilgrimage of pleasure will not be ended till at Niagara Falls we listen to the cataract's roar, and ascertain whether there is truth in the common report that Table Rock is " out of repair."

New York lies, like a Neapolitan lazzarone, with its head on the grass and its feet in the water. From Central Park to the Battery, ebb and flow the tides of city life. It is estimated that in the course of twenty-four hours, seventeen thousand vehicles pass the Astor House in Broadway, wearing out the stone block pavement once in fifteen years.

From the turf and flowers of Central Park to the waves which wash the Battery (and cannot wash it clean) may at the present hour be called the full stretch of the city. There are men not yet in the decline of life who can remember when the Astor House was quite an up-town institution, and it is very possible that *we* may live to behold Central Park located in the heart of New York city.

In population, New York already claims to rank as the third city of Christendom, and its rate of progress in the future is certain to be far greater than that of Paris, and likely to be somewhat greater than that of London.

How many of our city residents, or country friends visiting the city, have viewed the panorama to be seen from Trinity steeple? Let those who can do so, not fail to enjoy it. You ascend many steps, creep around amid the ponderous chimes, rusty, cavernous and solemn; then patiently wind round and round up the interior of the spire, with occasional lookouts, at which you may pause and get foretastes of the promised picture, and at last reach the top, or rather, the highest point of ascent, which is the uppermost window or loophole. The spire still stretches some fifty feet above. The view that opens before you is now really very fine. To the northward there is a wilderness of roofs, with spires and green-dotted parks, and Broadway's straight, wall-like line and stately marble warehouses, and, far away, the green hills of Westchester. At your feet is Wall street, and you wonder if you could not jump upon the dome of the Custom House. To the right, if you face southward, is the broad Hudson at its mouth, with the Jersey shore, and Communipaw, and the distant Orange hills. To the left is the swift East river, with Brooklyn beyond. Before you is the grand bay, with Staten Island, and the forts, and the islands, and the Narrows, and the great ocean beyond, whose offing is dotted with distant ships. And, added to this expansive panorama of town and river and ocean and shore, is the wonderful and varied picturesque animation of the scene. From below rises the " stilly hum" of the turbulent and restless city. Wall street, with its immense crowds of dark-coated men rushing hither and thither, looking like a vast hive whose inmates have been thrown into wild excitement by some unexpected intrusion ; and Broadway, packed thickly with its long line of interlocked vehicles ; then the river on either side, crowded with sails and busy ferry-boats, and lined by storehouses, ships and steamers ; and the grand bay, with anchored frigates, swift-moving yachts and puffing steamers ; all combine to make up a picture not easily matched, and, once seen, likely to be long remembered. Those of our readers who have not enjoyed this spectacle, would find the somewhat laborious ascent of the steeple amply rewarded by the result.

That brilliant writer, Justin McCarthy, declares that Broadway, the backbone of New York, is usually one of the brightest and most animated streets in the world. No two houses in all its vast length (and it is as if the Strand intersected London from end to end) are like each other ; this side of the street is never like that. A huge building of white marble stands next to one of brown stone, both of the newest and most glaring hues ; then comes a quaint old Dutch house of the days of Stuyvesant, and then again, something little better than a shanty.

On this side you are reminded now of the Rue de Rivoli; cast your eyes across the street and you see a scrap of the New Cut, or a bit of Wapping. Here a side street seems borrowed from Liverpool; a few yards on is another which appears to have been transplanted from Delft or Utrecht. The shop fronts glitter with signs and flutter with flags. A Chinese city is not more parti-colored, bright, eccentric and fantastic, in its buildings and insignia.

But our way lies *through* the Empire State. New York city is, in itself, a museum of wonders. Its attractions are countless. To enumerate them is to fill a volume. Yet, on summer days, none more than Americans make it a principle to desert the city, though none less than Americans know how to dispense with it. Leaving splendid Fifth avenue and squalid Five Points alike behind us, we will seek the foot of Vestry street, where the North River steamers occupy their well-known place in that water-belt of commerce which nearly surrounds the Island of Manhattan.

As the boat leaves its pier, a beautiful view is obtained of the the Upper Bay of New York. In the distance loom up the Highlands of Neversink—the last land which gladdens the eye of the ocean voyager.

Upon the opposite shore from New York lies JERSEY CITY. It was once known as Paulus Hook. Mighty tides of travel sweep daily through Jersey City. It is the highway leading to the Middle and Southern States. The dock of the Cunard line of steamers is also located here.

Farther up the shore is HOBOKEN, beyond which stretch the spreading lawns and luxuriant foliage of the Elysian Fields, *once* the famous and romantic resort of lovers; *now*, perhaps, equally dear to the devotees of base ball.

Weehawken Bluffs upon the north and Bergen Heights upon the west, give a wild background to this fair landscape of city and shore. The limit of Hoboken is the rocky promontory long known as Castle Hill, on which stands the mansion of the Stevens family.

Near Hoboken the little town of WEEHAWKEN acquires a gloomy consequence from the sad and mysterious murder of the "beautiful cigar girl."

We present in our pages a view of New York, from Weehawken, with its line of wharves and rows of warehouses, Trinity Church and the Battery in distinct view, beyond which are the walls of Castle William, on Governor's Island, and still further on, the waters of New York Bay, the Narrows, Long Island and Staten Island.

In striking contrast with this scene is the representation of New York, then known as Nieuw Amsterdam, in 1650, when our worthy Dutch ancestors held full sway between the East and North rivers and all along up the Hudson.

The picture of modern New York from Weehawken is taken, looking southward, from the spot where Hamilton fell by the bullet of Aaron Burr, in 1804.

Few strangers, says Mr. James Grant Wilson, came to New York fifty years ago without visiting the celebrated duelling-ground on the romantic bank of the Hudson, about two miles above the Hoboken Ferry. It was a grassy ledge, or shelf, about twenty feet above the water, and only sufficiently large for the fatal encounters that frequently occurred there in the old dueling days, being about two yards wide by twelve in length. From this celebrated spot there was a natural and almost regular flight of steps to the edge of the rocky shore where a landing was effected. This singularly-isolated and secluded spot was reached by small boats, being inaccessible to foot-passengers along the shore, except at very low tide. No path led to it from the picturesque heights of Weehawken, whose beauties have been sung by Halleck, and are familiar to all New Yorkers; but the ground was sometimes reached from above by adventurous persons who descended the steep, rough and wooded declivity.

It was to this spot that the fiery Tybalts resorted for the settlement of difficulties according to the " code of honor," prevailing at the beginning of the nineteenth century. Here occurred the meetings referred to by Byron, when he says:

> "It is a strange, quick jar upon the ear,
> That cocking of a pistol, when you know
> A moment more will bring the sight to bear
> Upon your person, twelve yards off, or so;
> A gentlemanly distance, not too near,
> If you have got a former friend for foe;
> But, after being fired at once or twice,
> The ear becomes more Irish and less nice."

It was at the Weehawken Dueling Ground that Philip Hamilton, at the age of twenty, was killed, November 23, 1801, in an " affair of honor," by George J. Eacker, who was, like his victim, a young lawyer of New York; it was here in the year following that a Mr. Bird was shot through the heart, and, springing up nearly ten feet, fell dead; here Ben Price was killed by a Captain Green of the British army; and it was on this celebrated ground that Alexander Hamilton fell, on the morning of July 11, 1804, on the very spot where his eldest son had been killed. Several months after the duel, the St. Andrew's Society, of whom the lamented patriot had been the president, erected upon the ground a marble monument, and surrounded it with an iron railing. Every summer thousands of strangers visited the spot. As the years glided past, the railing was torn down by vandal hands, and the whole structure gradually removed, piece by piece, as souvenirs, till at length no vestige of it remained. Two granite blocks inscribed with the names of Burr and Hamilton, deeply cut in the stone, and the former dated 1804, marked the spots where they stood face to face on that fatal July morning, sixty-seven years ago.

A few summers since we visited the romantic and secluded spot, in company with one who was well acquainted with all the actors in the tragedy, and who pointed out the positions of the principals, and the old cedar tree under which Hamilton stood, while the seconds, Judge Pendleton and Wm. P. Van Ness, were arranging the preliminaries, and Dr. David Hosack, Mr. Davis, and the boatmen sat in the boats, awaiting the result of the duel which ended so tragically. Perhaps, since the world began, no hostile meeting in an "affair of honor" ever created such an excitement—certainly no one that has occurred in this country—as the deadly encounter between Aaron Burr and Alexander Hamilton.

On a bright May morning of the present year we revisited the ancient dueling-ground, but alas, it had been swept out of existence by that "villainous alteration miscalled *improvement*." Nothing remains to mark the spot but a weather-beaten stone on which the name Hamilton has been almost obliterated by the winds and rains of heaven. In place of the narrow ledge, there is now a broad track over which the trains of the West-Side Railroad thunder northward to Fort Lee, and farther on, awakening the echoes from the picturesque Weehawken heights and the lofty Highlands of the Hudson.

"Let me hope, I pray you," wrote Fitz-Greene Halleck to a lady friend at Fort Lee, a few years ago, "that while I live you will not allow a person, whom I refrain from naming (the same person who entered, of old, the only paradise on earth to be compared to Fort Lee, in the shape of a rattle-snake, and played the very devil there), to come in the shape of a railroad locomotive, screaming his way through your garden, up to a crystal palace on the top of the Palisades, at the rate of forty miles an hour." The poet's prayer was realized; he did not live to witness this much-needed improvement, and to have his heart saddened by what he would have deemed a desecration of the fondly-cherished scene so indelibly impressed upon his memory.

The venerable cedar tree against which Hamilton leaned, as he gazed sadly, for the last time, on the distant city which held all that was dear to him in this world, has been cut down and thrown into the river, and the place changed beyond all recognition. Looking around for the memorials of past days, we at length discovered the granite block inscribed with the name of Hamilton; but the other was not to be found, nor the numerous rocks, which we had seen on a former visit, decorated with the names or initials of persons who had made pilgrimages to the place.

A gang of laborers were at work near the spot, and to their foreman we addressed an inquiry about the granite block inscribed " Burr, 1804." The conversation ran as follows :

" Have you seen here a large stone similar to this one marked Hamilton ? "

" Yes."

" Was it marked with the name of Burr, and dated 1804 ? "

" It was."

" Do you know where it is ? "

" Yes."

" Can you point it out to me ? "

" Well, I guess not, seeing it's underground. It's been used as a covering stone in a culvert just above here."

NEW YORK, 1650.

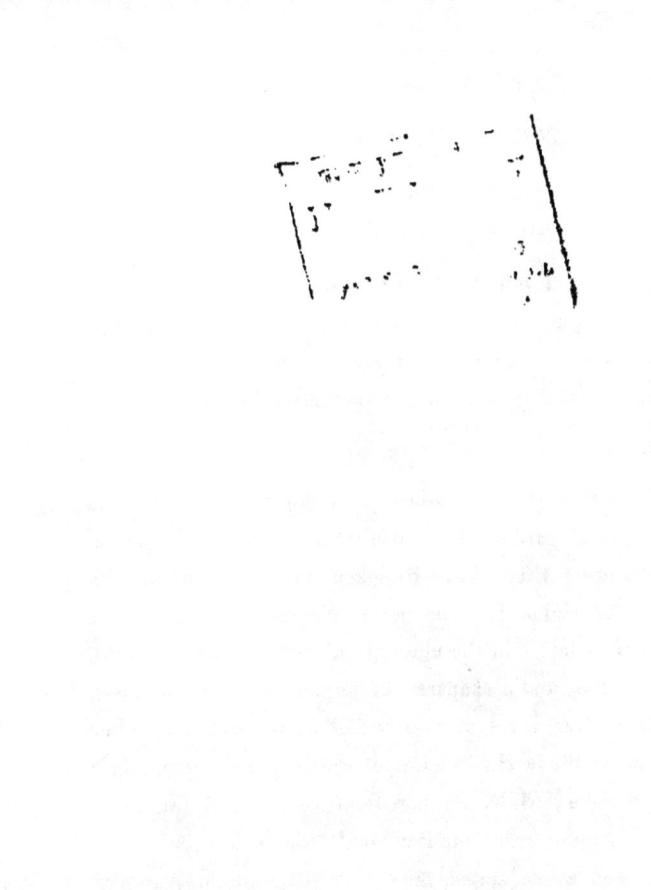

"Could you not have made use of another stone, and allowed the interesting memorial to remain?"

"Why, yes; and I told the boss he'd better lay it alongside of t'other stone; but he said that Burr was a mean cuss, anyhow, and not of much account, and he guessed it would be more useful doing duty as a covering stone than perpetuating his memory."

Such is life!!!

In this vicinity are the garden-beds—the flower nurseries of the metropolis. Floral gardeners monopolize the land all along from the rear of Hudson City, West Hoboken and the Teutonically-classic shades of Union Hill, as far as Weehawken. There are whole "beds of violets," in the most literal sense, forests of tulips, thickets of dahlias, and a chaparral of mignonette. As for roses, the celebrated seven acres of rose bushes on the South Carolina estate of General Wade Hampton, as it was before the war, might envy their profusion; while, for perennial beauty and fragrance, "the thrice-blooming roses of Pæstum," whose delicious odors enchanted Cicero as he sailed, far out at sea, past the Ausonian coast, could not surpass them. The Prince of Wales once sent to the Empress Eugenie, as a graceful acknowledgment for her attentions in Paris to his princess-consort, a bouquet containing no less than *fifty* rare varieties of the queen of flowers. Had he been in America, he would have no difficulty in surpassing this selection in the neighborhood of Union Hill.

Violets, roses, camelias, tuberoses, mignonette and heliotrope are sold in New York every year, to the value of nearly one and a half million dollars.

Hot-house culture is more largely carried on upon the eastern bank of the Hudson. This branch of the flower trade is immense, and will soon exceed the floral commerce of Holland, where six million flower-plants are sold annually.

WEEHAWKEN is also noted as the place where the Indians first became intoxicated, and, under the influence of "fire-water," gravely surmised that the Hudson must have become inebriated when it started on its career, or it would never have sought such a winding channel to the sea.

Pleasure grounds belonging to one of the "Summer Homes" lying on the Hudson's eastern shore.

NEW YORK TO IRVINGTON.

II.

AS New York recedes from view, the significant, upward-pointing finger of Trinity steeple will be the last noticeable object to be distinguished.

The history of "Old Trinity" is closely interwoven with the records of New York. It is the "rich church" of the land. Erected in 1696, *it then stood on the northern outskirts of the city.* It has been twice destroyed by fire. Fulton, the inventor of steam navigation, sleeps in its churchyard. Near him rests Lawrence, whose last words—"Don't give up the ship"—will be remembered while the love of country animates patriot breasts. There, too, a plain, simple monument, erected by a noble English lady, commemorates the dust of "Charlotte Temple," whose pitiful story was whispered and wept over, two generations ago.

There, too, rises the handsome tomb which was erected to our fallen Brave, for the double purpose of honoring the dead and preventing Albany and Pine streets from being cut through the yard—an amusing combination of motives, it must be confessed.

The tourist who travels by boat instinctively looks backward. Maidens and matrons, men of pleasure and of business, alike cast interested glances over this receding vista of one of the young giant cities of the world. Those who journey in the train of the iron horse, if they are philosophical, may recall the fact, that the road by which they travel is but one line of a railway network extending over the country, the sum total of whose meshes foots up over *fifty thousand miles*. More timid souls ponder on " a sermon with a *smash up* for a text "—and the nonchalant are devoted to that absorbing American idol, the inevitable newspaper.

Steamboat travelers feel both more secure and more at leisure than those who ride by rail. It is only upon the Mississippi now-a-days that
> "A nigger is squat on the safety-valve,
> And the furnace crammed with rosin and pine!"

The day line of steamers plying between New York and Albany proffer attractions and advantages which are seldom combined in one route of equal length. Historical associations and old romantic traditions linger along the banks where
> " Hudson's wave o'er silvery sands,
> Winds thro' the hills afar."

Evidences of the fashion and the prosperity of to-day are also visible on every hand.

The boats of the Day Line, namely, the well-known C. Vibbard and the Daniel Drew, are, probably, without exception, the swiftest steamboats in the world. Built especially to meet the requirements of summer travel on the Hudson, these boats combine qualities of speed and comfort with ample facilities for viewing the magnificent scenery through which they pass. The two boats are essentially the same in size and equipments. The dimensions of the Vibbard are as follows:

Length of keel... 265 feet
Breadth of beam... 34 "
Depth of hold...9 feet 8 inches
Diameter of cylinder..... .... 62 "
Length of stroke... 12 feet

The highest speed ever attained by these boats was made by the Vibbard, which went from New York to Tarrytown, a distance of twenty-seven miles, in one hour. The same boat has also run from West Point to Newburg, ten miles, in twenty and one-half minutes. This speed was made on an extraordinary occasion, however, and the powers of the boats are not so severely tested when carrying passengers.

The Day Boats leave Pier 39, North River, at the foot of Vestry street, at 8:30 A. M., touching, fifteen minutes later, at Thirty-fourth street, and reaching Albany at 6 o'clock P. M., landing at the foot of Hamilton street, and connecting with the Chicago Express on the New York Central Railroad, and the Susquehanna Railroad. Upon their return trips they leave Albany at 9 A. M., reaching New York at 6:15 P. M.

Upon the Daniel Drew a very good story is told, for the truth of which we will not vouch, that " Uncle Daniel," as he is familiarly known in Wall street, once went on board the boat which bears his name, in what could not be truthfully described as " stunning" attire, and was accosted by a passenger, who mistook him for an employee, with, "Well, do you belong to the boat ?" " No, sir," was the quiet reply, " *the boat belongs to me.*" Whether true or not, it is a good story to tell of the Wall street financier, and we suspect that, like many histories, " it is founded on fact."

The traveler who deems it preferable to leave New York at night, will find the steamers Vanderbilt and Connecticut, of the New York and Troy Line, extremely elegant, commodious and well-managed. These boats are swift and strong, and run between Troy, Albany and New York, in connection with the Rensselaer and Saratoga, Troy and Boston roads, Albany and Susquehanna, and New York Central railroads. Their departures and arrivals are timed to accommodate passengers by all these routes, and Hudson River Railroad tickets, if desired, are received for passage, including stateroom. The liberal management of this line secures for it a large share of public patronage and favor.

In the TOURIST GUIDE we present the western shore of the Island of Manhattan, as it was depicted by an early artist, not long after the advent of the Colonists, and ere the hand of man had effaced or altered the work of Nature's hand.

How changed is the scene which is spread out before the gaze of the traveler now!

The PALISADES commence at Weehawken, although they do not attain their most majestic height for several miles. They run northward about twenty miles, a sheer wall of rock varying from two hundred to six hundred feet in height, surmounted by a fringe of forest trees. The form of these cliffs and the slope beneath them to the water, is similar to that of the vaunted cliffs upon the northern coast of Ireland. They command an exquisite view of the Hudson river and its shores upon the east, and of the fields of New Jersey upon the west—for Fort Lee, be it remembered, is not part and parcel of the Empire State, but is included in the survey of Bergen county, N. J.

But we must speed on to FORT LEE, which lies on the western bank of the river, ten miles from the City Hall. The remains of the fort are scarcely discernible. It was here that the Continental Congress ordered the obstruction of the navigation of the river by "every art and at whatever expense." It was thus that plucky

MANHATTAN ISLAND 1609.

Americans waged unequal but victorious war with British foes. The Palisades are here three hundred feet high. Country seats are already in process of erection along the brow of the Palisades.

MANHATTANVILLE is a part of New York. The name is given to the neighborhood of 132d street. A little south of Manhattanville, in the neighborhood of 117th street, the Lunatic Asylum occupies a fine, elevated location. It is surrounded by about forty acres of ornamental grounds. This asylum, better known as the Bloomingdale Hospital, has been the retreat of the ruined and brain-crazed speculators of Wall street, to a greater extent, perhaps, than any other institution in the country. Here, too, the daughter of a Senator, and wife of an ex-Governor of one of the Southern States, for many years played the *role* of Queen Elizabeth. She was dressed always in pure white, and is said to have been, of all lunatic queens, the most beautiful and the happiest.

Nearer the river is the Claremont Hotel, which was the home of Joseph Bonaparte during the first year of his exile in this country. Manhattan College, a Catholic institution, the Convent of the Ladies of the Sacred Heart, and the Colored Orphan Asylum, are all in this vicinity.

CARMANSVILLE, at 152d street, is another of the suburbs of New York. Here, for many years, lived Audubon, the most distinguished of American ornithologists, whose fame chiefly rests upon his splendid volume, " The Birds of America," which was issued in 1828, for one hundred and seventy subscribers, at $1,000 per copy. In 1833, upon his last return from Europe, he purchased the estate which he called " Minnie's Land." It is now known as Audubon Park, and the house still exists. Audubon died in 1848, and is interred in Trinity Cemetery, near by—that City of the Dead, after another made additions to it, till the present structure was completed. Even its friends admit that it is "architecturally inharmonious;" we will not repeat what its critics say.

We reach YONKERS next. It is a thriving suburban town. A few years ago New Yorkers went to Yonkers to obtain "summer board," but now the denizens of Yonkers visit "the country" in the heated term, and Yonkers in August is almost as deserted as the city itself. The name Yonkers is derived from the Dutch Yonk-heer, signifying the heir of a family. For many years it has been repeated and believed, that Washington's "first love" was the fair Mary Philipse, of this town, but the modern historians, who have nearly proved Mary of Scots,

"Less to be pitied than blamed,"

and have robbed the story of Pocahontas of its heroic pathos, now affirm that Washington never knelt at the shrine of the belle of Yonkers. It cannot be denied, however, that the Philipse Manor House is an existing *fact*. It is a stone building erected in 1682, with the addition of its front in 1745. It is owned by Mr. Woodworth, who is surely "the right man in the right place," for his efforts tend to preserve unchanged this interesting memorial of

"Ye olden times."

The bold mariner, Hendrick Hudson, anchored off Yonkers when ascending the Hudson in September, 1609. Here, the record runs, that he found a "loving people, who attained great age." An illustration given in our pages represents his ship, the "Half Moon," at anchorage, while the boats of the Indians ply between it and the shore. Hendrick Hudson's face also appears in this scene, and is a copy of the original portrait, painted in 1592, and many years since presented to the State of New York by one of its oldest families, of Dutch descent. The painting is of undoubted authenticity, and may be seen in the City Hall of New York.

HASTINGS-ON-THE-HUDSON, three miles north of Yonkers, is the home of many New York families. When Garibaldi was keeping his soap and candle factory on Staten Island, and resided there, he used to spend his Sundays here with Italian friends, most of whom were prominent musical artists in the Italian Opera. A friend, living at Dobb's Ferry, an accomplished student and enthusiastic lover of Italian literature, often entertained him at dinner. Garibaldi is represented by those who met him at this time as a finely-formed man, self-possessed, with a face of striking intelligence, and great modesty of manner. He was well versed in the works of Italy's great authors, and discussed them in excellent English—very quiet, unconsequential, speaking from a full mind when he did speak, and saying nothing when he could not.

DOBBS' FERRY next introduces us to the land of tradition. The legends of the Hudson are numberless. They were once told at every hearthside, though now they are passing from remembrance. Our busy, care-laden people allow the STATISTICS of to-day to crowd upon the legends of the past, yet the "Fairy of Dobbs' Ferry" will undoubtedly long hold a place in the memorial book of the Hudson.

The romantic story of an interrupted wedding and a lost bride, for whom unavailing search is made, is concluded by the advent of a Fay

"Leading Katrina thro' the ruined halls."

A kiss reunites the separated lovers, who were both transformed into fairies.

"And still some people of that section say,
That when the stars roll in their middle way,
The immortal pair amid the ruins stand,
Just as they should be, *always hand in hand!*"

We believe there are other versions of this legend, some of which allow Hendrick and Katrina to

"Live out their days
In more common ways;"

but we " tell the tale as 'twas told to us ! "

Dobbs' Ferry was also christened in blood during the black days of the Revolution. It was here, also, that the first meeting of Arnold with Andre was appointed to take place, but it proved unsuccessful. And here, too, the English, forgetting the *fearful and fatal precedents* they had given us, made unavailing intercession for the life of their brave but unfortunate Spy.

PIERMONT lies almost opposite, and near the line between New York and New Jersey. Here the Palisades recede from the shore and lose their precipitous character. The ridge continues, however, in a series of hills, reaching, in some places, a height of nearly seven hundred feet, but nowhere resuming the peculiar formation of the Palisades. It is curious to remark, that for nearly thirty miles up the Hudson, the western shore presents either some variety of trap rock, conglomerate, or secondary foundation, while the eastern shore abounds in granite or primitive rock, as also the entire Island of Manhattan. Piermont derives its name from its pier, one mile in length. It was once a branch and is now a main terminus of the Erie railroad. A fine, broad Boulevard is now being opened from Piermont to Rockland Lake, seven miles distant, passing the pretty town of Nyack, and forming a delightful addition to the pleasant drives in this vicinity.

Not far from Piermont lies the old town of Tappan, where Major Andre was tried, condemned and executed. Washington often made this place his headquarters during the Revolution. The house of the commander-in-chief and the jail in which Andre was imprisoned, may be seen here, although the same practical spirit which in old Salem has transformed the court-room where the terrible death sentence was pronounced upon the luckless witches of that day, into a grocery store, has in Tappan converted the jail into a public house known as the Seventy-six Stone House. The old Dutch church in which Andre was tried, stood near by, but was replaced by a new edifice in 1836. The place of his execution is within a short walk of the old Stone House.

III.

RVINGTON bears a memorial name, and must always be a place of interest to every American. It was formerly known as Dearman's Station. It is four miles north of Dobbs' Ferry, and communicates by ferry with Piermont, on the opposite shore.

Between Dobbs' Ferry and Irvington is Nevis, once the homestead of Colonel James Hamilton. It contains many records of the olden time, among which is the portrait of Washington, taken by Stuart, which is considered the best likeness, and has been the most widely copied, of any of his portraits. Very near Nevis is the home of Mr. Cottinet, built of Caen stone, and frequently pronounced the most elegant residence on the Hudson.

Bierstadt, the artist, has a fine villa at Irvington. The house is of stone, and is provided with a large studio.

Every year adds to the list of men of *note*, as well as men of wealth—the two are not always synonymous—who seek homes upon the picturesque banks of this noble stream, of which Irving said: " The Hudson is, in a manner, my first and last love; and, after all my wanderings and seeming infidelities, I return to it with a heart-felt preference over all the rivers of the world."

The Hudson is often compared with the Rhine, but one of the most discriminating of travelers, George William Curtis, pronounces the Hudson larger and grander than the Rhine. "The Hudson, says he, "implies a continent behind. For vineyards, it has forests; for a belt of water, a majestic stream. The Danube has, in parts, glimpses of such grandeur. The Elbe has sometimes such delicately pencilled effects. But no European river is so lordly in its bearing, none flows in such state to the sea." Yet different people view the same streams and scenes with very diverse emotions.

An industrious Scotchman, who had accumulated a very handsome property, recently sent to the "auld countrie" for his father, with a view that he should share his prosperity, and slip away from his lease of life as smoothly as possible. One day a friend of the family paid a visit to the elegant mansion on the Hudson, where the old gentleman was living with his son, and took occasion to compliment the proprietor of the estate on its surpassing loveliness and cozy comfort. The owner, full of love for his beautiful home, said he looked upon it and its surroundings as "a perfect heaven on earth." "Heaven on earth!" growled the venerable Scot, "heaven on earth, and no' a thimblefu' o' whuskey in the haill house!"

Sunny Side, the residence of the late Washington Irving, is at once a poet's cottage lost in verdure and flowers, and a reminiscence of olden time. The house abounds in relics of the old Dutch style. A venerable weathercock, of portly dimensions—we are informed by Irving in the Knickerbocker—"which once battled with the wind on the top of the Stadt-house of New Amsterdam, in the time of Peter Stuyvesant, now erects his crest on the gable end of my edifice. A gilded horse, in full gallop, once the weathercock of the great Van der Heyden palace of Albany, glitters in the sunshine and veers with every breeze, on the peaked turret over my portal."

The Melrose ivy which embowers the eastern side of the cottage, is a memento of the friendship of two great men—Walter Scott and Washington Irving—the earlier slips having been presented by Sir Walter, and planted by the hand of Irving himself. The original house was built by Wolfert Acker, in the days of the Dutch Governors, and bore over the door the inscription "Lust in Rust," the meaning of which is "pleasure in quiet."

It was to this pleasant retreat that Mr. Irving came to find a home, soon after his return to this country, in 1832, after an absence of seventeen years from his native land, and having won a world-wide fame for himself and for American literature. At that time Irving and Cooper were the only American authors whose names were known in Europe.

A bust of Irving was taken about this time by Mr. Ball Hughes, which has been considered by his friends a satisfactory likeness. A colossal bust, by Macdonald, has been ordered by a liberal citizen, for Prospect Park, Brooklyn, and bids fair to be a remarkable success, showing Mr. Irving as he was in mature age, ere his health failed.

Is it not time that our beautiful Central Park, which has been long ornamented with a bust of Schiller, should possess a sculptured memorial of Irving and Cooper? One of Mr. Irving's visitors at the "Roost"—afterwards re-christened Sunnyside—was a young foreigner, then boarding in New York at the popular hotel which stood on the site of Stewart's down-town store. This guest

MINUITS' PURCHASE OF THE ISLAND OF MANHATTAN.

has since been known as Emperor Napoleon III., and as the man of Sedan. It does not appear that the horoscope of the youth was cast at the cottage, or that his future elevation and downfall were even guessed at there. In 1853, however, Mr. Irving wrote thus significantly: " Napoleon and Eugenie, Emperor and Empress! The one I have had as a guest at my cottage, the other I have held as a pet child upon my knee in Granada. The last I saw of Eugenie Montijo, she was one of the reigning belles of Madrid; and she and her giddy circle had swept away my charming friend, the beautiful and accomplished ——, into their career of fashionable dissipation. Now, Eugenie is upon the throne, and —— is a voluntary recluse in a convent of one of the most rigorous orders. Poor ——! Perhaps, however, her fate may ultimately be the happiest of the two. 'The storm with her is o'er and she's at rest,' *but the other is launched from a returnless shore, upon a dangerous sea, infamous for its tremendous shipwrecks.* Am I to live to see the catastrophe of her career, and the end of this suddenly conjured up empire, which seems to be of such stuff as dreams are made of. I confess my personal acquaintance with the individuals in this historical romance gives me uncommon interest in it; but I consider it stamped with danger and instability, and as liable to extravagant vicissitudes as one of Dumas' novels."

There may be no profound sagacity or special gift of prophecy in these surmises, but they are curiously in accordance with the *finale* of 1870, which the seer did *not* live to see.

It was at Sunnyside, also, that Daniel Webster, then Secretary of State, paid a visit in 1842, giving Mr. Irving the unexpected information of his appointment as Minister to Spain. This compliment seems to have been due to the influence of Mr. Webster alone, and it is pleasant to see one man of intellect thus render homage to another. Nor is it alone with the more highly endowed that the classic annalist of New York has won his fame. Prior to January 1st, 1857, the aggregate sale of Irving's works in America was about 500,000 volumes. This estimate does not include 98,000 volumes of the " Life of Washington," sold to January, 1857, nor the large sales of " Woolfert's Roost." The sale of Irving's writings exceed what has been claimed for the works called " sensation books," and is creditable to the taste of the nation. At Sunnyside were written all of his later books, many noted guests were entertained there, and a most honored and stainless life was lived out to its end. On a gray, November day, with the Bible open near him, which had once belonged to that fair betrothed, for whose dear sake he had lived unmated full fifty years, he went to join *her*, where lovers shall be no more separated, by time, and change, and death, before the Throne of God.

A long procession followed Irving to his grave over a road which winds through " Sleepy Hollow," and there he will sleep till the " Heavens be no more."

TARRYTOWN lies north of Irvington, twenty-nine miles from New York. Let the stranger land there, or step from the cars as we did once, not far from noon, upon a blazing summer day, and ere he completes a stroll through the town, he will conclude that he has found " Sleepy Hollow," indeed. There is an absence of the Yankee element of hurry, which is very restful to the spirit. The air of dolce far niente, which seems to pervade the place, might be exasperating, under some circumstances, to a busy man—but do busy men ever set foot in Tarrytown, except when they have leisure to take summer holiday? It is an open question which we will leave those wiser than ourselves to discuss and settle. Meanwhile the Editor locks up his newspaper office and goes home to dinner;

the grocer falls asleep; somebody gravely tells you that Broadway, the pride of Tarrytown, is "just a continuation of Broadway, New York, which comes all the way up here"—which you incline to doubt, and—if it is June, the breezes are more odorous of sweet syringa blossoms than any breezes of city or country which you ever enjoyed before. This is Tarrytown and there are superb drives here. A "team" seems to be owned by everybody, for no one that you can see goes a-foot. Hack fare is paid by "a quarter" in postal currency, and the hired carriage rumbles contentedly along, distanced by more than one city coach with drivers in livery.

That painful uniformity of architecture, which is so noticeable in some of the river towns, does not meet you here. Taste and wealth have not only reared many elegant homes, but have perched many most beautiful residences on the hill-side, whence they look down, as from an eyrie, upon the town—on the old Dutch Church and famous Sleepy Hollow.

The *Show Place* of Tarrytown is the white marble edifice known as the Paulding Manor, which stands just below the town. It was built by the descendants of Commodore Paulding, and is one of the finest specimens of the pointed Tudor style of domestic architecture in the United States. It is also the most conspicuous dwelling to be seen by the traveler on the Lower Hudson.

It seems singular to us that, among all the writers who have visited and written of Sleepy Hollow, so few have, within our knowledge, described, in fitting terms, the extreme beauty of the *hillside landscape*, which lends enchantment to the background of any view of the town and valley.

Upon Broadway stands a fine monument, erected by the people of Westchester county, October 7th, 1853, with this inscription:

<blockquote>
On this spot,
The 23d day of September, 1780, the Spy,
MAJOR JOHN ANDRE,
Adjutant General of the British Army, was
Captured by
JOHN PAULDING, DAVID WILLIAMS AND ISAAC VAN WART,
All natives of this country.
History has told the rest.
</blockquote>

It is a curious fact, and one not generally known, that the tree beneath which Andre was captured was finally smitten by lightning in July, 1801, on the *very day* of Benedict Arnold's death in London. Our American poets have often drawn inspiration from far less suggestive themes than this.

Another singular incident relates to a cypress tree which grew for many years above Andre's grave. In 1832 a vessel was sent to this country by the order of George IV., to convey the remains of Andre to England to be reinterred in Westminster Abbey. The roots of this cypress tree were found entwined around the skull of poor Andre, and a slip from the tree was carried to England and planted in the gardens adjoining Windsor Castle. A scion from that slip now flourishes in a garden walk which has been a favorite resort with Queen Victoria, and the young bride, Lady Lorne. Still another tree must be mentioned in this list, of those which are now the only living links between us and the remote past.

A few years ago the almost lifeless remains of a huge willow tree stood on the border of a marsh near Beverly Dock, in the Hudson Highlands, almost opposite West Point. It was known as Arnold's Willow, because it was there, a flourishing tree, before treason clouded his reputation. It stood by the side of the pathway by which he fled from his headquarters to the river, when his treachery was revealed, late in September, 1780.

Arnold's flight was precipitous and perilous. A stupid officer, who did not comprehend the case, wrote to Arnold of the arrest of

Andre. The traitor was well aware that papers were in Andre's possession, the discovery of which would seal his doom with the stern patriots of '76. He bade his wife a hasty farewell, kissed the babe in her arms, and then fled at full gallop down the lane, by the old Willow Tree to the shore. His barge was in readiness; and, bidding the oarsmen pull southward with all their strength, for his business was urgent, he escaped to the British sloop-of-war Vulture, then lying in Tappan Bay.

Major Andre was executed as a spy; but Arnold lived twenty years to feel the tortures of a troubled conscience and the bitter scorn of his fellow-men. He had attempted to sell the liberties of his country for the commission of a brevet-brigadier in the British army, and fifty thousand dollars in gold.

Those whom he had served loathed and scorned him. Cornwallis would not associate with him in Virginia; and in England even the Government could not gain him recognition in society.

> " From Cain to Cataline, the world hath known
> Her Traitors—vaunted votaries of crime—
> Caligula and Nero sat alone
> Upon the pinnacle of vice sublime ;
> But they were moved by hate, or wish to climb
> The rugged steeps of Fame, in letters bold
> To write their name upon the scroll of Time ;
> Therefore their crimes some virtue did enfold—
> But Arnold ! thine had none—'twas all for sordid gold."

We deem there are none so stern of heart, or so indifferent that they can reflect on the fate of Andre, without a sentiment of pity. It was known that early disappointment in love impelled that accomplished young man to enter the army. This circumstance increased the sympathy felt for him more than ninety years ago. Andre's appeal to Washington that he might *die a soldier's death*, doubtless touched the great heart of the 'Father of his

Country,' as deeply as if it had been couched in Willis' poetical version, at a later date, of Andre's request.

> " THINE is the power to give—
> Thine to deny—
> Peace for the hour to live,
> Calmness to die!"

But in deploring the stern necessity of war, which sent Andre to the gallows, let us not forget how Nathan Hale had previously died for his country. He was, perhaps, the best educated young man who left the halls of Yale for the camp of the patriot army. In attempting to return to the American lines he was seized and brought before Sir William Howe, who ordered him to be executed the next morning, and the sentence was carried into most barbarous effect. He asked if he might see a friend and was denied. He asked for a Bible and was refused. Even his last request, that a clergyman might visit him, was rejected with *oaths*. What a striking contrast to the conduct of Washington, who signed Andre's death warrant, with tears. More cruel, if possible, than all we have narrated above—Hale's letters, written the night before his death, to his mother and other dear friends, were broken open and burned, that the *rebels* might not know there was a man in their army who could die with so much firmness. We have also heard that " she who would been his bride went with her father at night through the British lines, took his body from the gibbet and carried it home."

Will not all this extenuate the fate of Andre, and tell us, in part, what *price was paid for freedom.*

Only in part, however, for. there are patriots living to-day, who can *well* remember months passed in Libby Prison, when a death like Andre's or Hale's would have been enviable—there are nameless graves at Andersonville and elsewhere, around which gather more surpassing horrors.

Thus we muse at that monument upon that old post road, which commemmorates the fidelity of three humble men, who said to Andre, " Not for ten thousand guineas could you stir one single step."

We crave your pardon, fair reader, for moralizing so long, but a blue sky and balmy air, and an after-dinner hour favoring you, at the same spot, we will wager a new History, or a set of Irving's works, that your thoughts will tread the same " busy backward track" that ours have done.

It is a long walk, or a short drive around to the Old Dutch Church, erected in 1615. It stands in the veritable Sleepy Hollow.

In its cemetery a very humble stone marks Irving's grave.

But the back window of the church is open. A fallen gravestone is so placed as to suggest, that by its aid some one has ascertained whether the interior is as antique as the quaint exterior of the old place of worship.

We are sorry to admit that we avail ourselves of the suggestion, but *not* sorry that we obtain a glance inside the church.

Leaving this quiet spot, we proceed along the country road towards the village, and not far from Sleepy Hollow notice the fine buildings and pleasant grounds of the Jackson Military Institute. As good schools are rare, we venture to say what we *know* of this one, that it is commended by some of the best men in the country, and that parents and guardians are welcomed here at all seasons, and afforded every opportunity of knowing exactly what manner of training—mental, physical and moral—*our boys* receive here.

The Principal of this Institute, some three years since, removed his institution to this place from Danbury, Conn., where it had borne a most successful record for twelve years.

There are few persons who visit Tarrytown, at least upon a summer's day, who will be able to leave it without reluctance. Yet regrets will be forgotten by those who have leisure to cross the river to Nyack.

NYACK-ON-THE-HUDSON, lying opposite Tarrytown, and accessible by a very commodious ferryboat, is one of the *gems* among the pleasant towns which lie on the Hudson's banks.

Tarrytown, with its old romance, its tragic story of Andre, its associations with the name of Irving, its guard over Irving's honored dust—its Sleepy Hollow and its Broadway—its old houses and its fine modern residences, has become well known to the traveling public.

In comparison with the multitudes who visit or pass through Tarrytown, Nyack is little frequented, yet there are those—and their number is increasing every year—who have discovered that Nyack is one of the most delightful and healthful of all the places of resort upon the river. It is also very easily accessible from New York city. There are consumptive people who have come here, regained their vigor, and lived out long lives. The west bank of the Hudson will soon dispute the palm with Minnesota as a retreat for invalids. It would have done so long ago were it not that a prophet lacks not honor, *save* in his own country. The views from Nyack are not so commanding as those which are obtained from West Point, but they are, nevertheless, grand, inspiriting and joyous.

Trains which leave the foot of Chambers street, New York, nine times daily, communicate with Nyack. In summer weather,

PALISADES.

Nyack is so easily and pleasantly reached by steamboat, that the business man may go to the city and return to Nyack every night, suffering no interruption to his business. There are, comparatively, so few places *where summer board is desirable, which are really easy of access* from New York, that we call especial attention to *Smith's Steamboat Line*, which runs three commodious boats daily from New York, touching at Yonkers, and nearly all places between Yonkers and Peekskill. The Nyack ferryboat meets these steamers in the middle of the river, and the transfer of passengers is effected with such ease and good humor that it seems a pleasant episode of the trip, rather than that usually much-dreaded and hateful thing—*a change*. Nyack is destined to become a very popular summer resort. Every year brings a larger throng of guests and sees additions made to the number of residences erected there by New York people. But Nyack is *not yet spoiled* for those who love the country. Prices have not gone up to balance Saratoga rates. The kindliness of a genial and refined people is not absorbed in that mania for money-getting which is so painfully perceptible at some of the older and better known resorts upon the river. Yet city comforts are abundant here. Gas has superseded that country abomination, kerosene. Rockland Lake Ice carts jog around composedly. Boating can be had. Bathing is good. Riding attainable at reasonable rates. The Smithsonian House, near the steamboat landing, is airy, commodious, and well furnished throughout, kept by a lady who has long been popular with those who can appreciate a well-kept house, where they can feel perfectly at home. We commend the comforts of the Smithsonian, from personal experience.

Guests are made welcome there, whether their stay is longer or shorter.

Then, too, the Clarendon, at a little distance, bears an excellent reputation, and is conducted by Mrs. Adams, who has had twenty years successful experience in St. Paul, Minnesota. We should add to these desirable places of resort, that *during the season* the Rockland Female Institute offers fine accommodations to summer boarders.

The Institute lies just beyond the village. This fine academic and collegiate school for young ladies was incorporated in 1855 by the Regents of the University of the State of New York, and opened for the reception of pupils the following year.

It was the design of its Founders to establish a Female Seminary of the highest order, which should furnish all the facilities for acquiring a substantial and finished education. In prosecution of this purpose they selected one of the most beautiful sites on the banks of the Hudson, and have expended about fifty thousand dollars upon the buildings and grounds.

The trustees state that in selecting Nyack as the seat of this Institution, they were not governed exclusively by regard for the wants of Rockland County, from which it derives its name, but by a conviction of its remarkable adaptation by nature for the purposes of a seminary of learning.

We invite you, reader, to stroll with us from the village to the Institute upon a summer evening. Boldly the noble building rises before us, five stories in height and one hundred feet in length, a fair and stately structure surrounded by noble trees, which reflect honor upon the Principal of the Institute, and do credit to the soil of Rockland County. They were planted by Rev. Mr. Mansfield —their growth is due to the fertility of mother earth, and the benificence of Heaven's dews and sunshine.

It is a lovely walk or drive from the village to the Institute. Upon one side lies that beautiful expanse of the Hudson, four miles wide, which is known as Tappan Zee. Upon the other rise the mountains, which in an inland and less precipitous form, are a continuation of the Palisades. We stand upon a semi-circular plateau surrounded on *all* sides by scenery of rare grandeur and beauty, while the summer sky is over all.

There are about ten acres in the grounds of the Institute—large gardens yield fruit and vegetables for its table. From half a bushel to a bushel of strawberries in their season, ripen every day, and these luxuries are placed before the pupils of the school. Happy school girls! Who would not become a pupil there—in strawberry time? Through the summer, boating, bathing and horseback riding can be enjoyed without leaving the grounds of the Institute—quite a number of ponies are kept for the use of the young ladies. In winter, skating and sleigh-riding; and all the year round, gymnastic exercises are in favor.

There are advantages in this location which cannot be obtained at a greater distance from the metropolis. Pupils visit New York with ease, under the charge of their teachers, enjoying the art galleries and other attractions of the city. A station upon the Nyack and Northern Railroad having been erected upon a portion of the Institute grounds, trips are made in one hour from Mansfield avenue, Nyack, to New York. This same depot, by the way, was designed by the Principal of the Institute, and is a model of elegance and good taste. Of the purely intellectual advantages of this school it is scarcely within our province to speak, but we may venture to say that the predictions of the high stand which this school would take among similar institutions, uttered by the Rev. Henry Ward Beecher, and others, when its present Principal assumed his charge, have been, in popular estimation, abundantly verified.

This is not a "high pressure" school, where delicate girls are taught every known "ology"—the standard of culture is high, however, and some of the most charming young ladies in the country have graduated here.

But we are lingering too long in Nyack—fair and favored spot—West Point and the Catskills lie northward. Let us journey on.

Between Nyack and Haverstraw is Rockland, whose oval lake on the hill furnishes ice for New York. It is upon a commanding height, known by a name which must have puzzled the orthographists of olden times—Verdrieteges Hook, which has such a deceptive appearance, viewed from the river above and below, of a grand headland, that it has been christened Point-no-Point. The original name signifies "grievous," given in consequence of the frequent squalls which beset the sailor in this neighborhood.

We opine that there are other Points, along the Hudson which will be called "grievous" by visitors, on summer nights, when little, stuffy rooms and kerosene lights, feather beds and mosquitoes, conspire to make up the sum of human evils.

We will not indicate further where such "summer board" may be found, save to say that where the landlord's bills are the highest in proportion to the accommodations offered, *there* look out for mosquito bills of unusual severity and power.

HAVERSTRAW is a pretty little village, where, upon what is known as "Treason Hill," stands the house of Joshua Hett Smith, where Andre and Benedict Arnold met to arrange the terms of the surrender of West Point. It is of stone, with a piazza in front, and stands on the hillside beyond the flats. Above Haver-

ROCKLAND FEMALE INSTITUTE.

straw is a line of limestone cliff about half a mile in length, and very valuable, producing a million bushels of lime every year, besides stone for rough masonry, and for macadamizing roads.

Directly opposite Haverstraw is SING SING. Many fine country seats crown the Heights of Sing Sing, and a number of educational establishments are located here. The great Croton Acqueduct at this point is very interesting, being carried over the Sing Sing Kill by an arch of stone masonry 88 feet between the abutments, and 100 feet above the water.

The mouth of Croton River is in this vicinity. The name is derived from an Indian word signifying " stony place."

The State Prison is a little south of the village and close by the banks of the Hudson. This is not the first instance of the erection of a prison commanding a fine water prospect, for Byron wrote :

" Loch Leman lies by Chillon's walls."

The prisoners are guarded by sentinels, in place of being enclosed by walls. The whole area of the grounds comprises about 130 acres. The railway passes through and beneath the prisons, but from the river they are seen to advantage.

The annual Camp Meetings of the Methodist Episcopal Church of New York and vicinity, which, for thirty-six years have been held at Sing Sing, add, in the summer time, an element of absorbing interest to the attractions of the town.

About three hundred tents are yearly occupied by families from New York and from towns along the Hudson River. Many improvements were made on the ground last year. Gas was introduced, and a reservoir of water was constructed, capable of holding 7,000 gallons. The water is conducted from a spring through galvanized iron pipes.

The arrangements for comfort, it is expected, will be carried still further toward perfection in the present summer.

CROTON POINT, four miles above Sing Sing, on the eastern bank of the Hudson, is noted for its famous lake, and its almost equally famous vineyard.

For more than thirty years the name of Dr. Underhill, of Croton Point, Westchester County, has been a household word in connection with the finest grapes in the market. For seventeen years this successful cultivator of the grape, laid aside an annual stock of pure wine—the genuine undoctored juice of the best grapes in the country, before a single bottle of it was offered for sale. For ten years past Underhill's wines have been known as *the* pure grape wines, superior to all others made in this country; they are recommended by some four hundred prominent medical men in New York city, and have received the approval of the invalid and the connoisseur everywhere. The Croton Point vineyards, owned by the late Dr. Underhill, cover an area of over sixty acres, and the yield is from 7,000 to 8,000 gallons of wine per annum, besides several tons of fruit sent directly to market. None of these wines are offered for sale until they are over four years old. And we hope that such wines as these—the pure juice of the grape—may drive out the "doctored" wines, with foreign names and domestic origin, which (dis)grace so many tables.

Visitors can reach Croton Dam by carriages from Sing Sing, from Croton, and from Croton Falls upon the Harlem road. This celebrated dam is 250 feet long, 40 feet high, and 70 feet thick at the base. The capacity of the Lake is 500,000,000 gallons. Another and much larger reservoir is now nearly completed, and it is anticipated that, when it is finished, all danger of suffering from scarcity of water in time of drouth will be obviated.

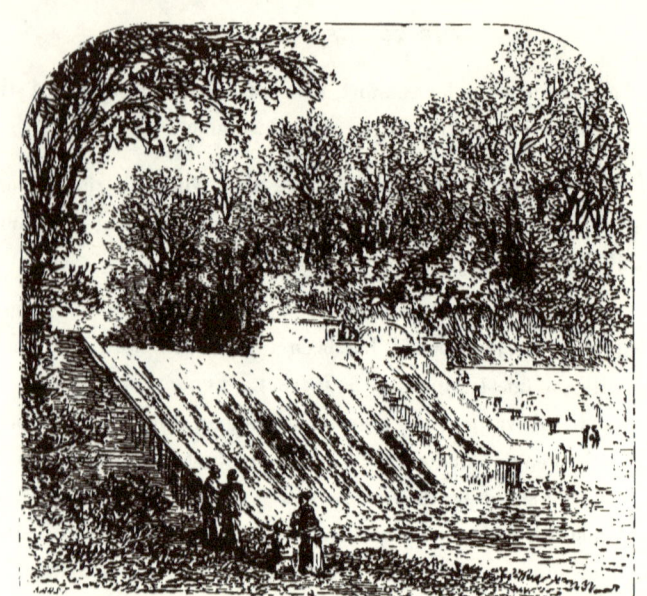

CROTON DAM.

We are conscious that we are what a school-girl would call "dreadfully statistical" along here, but Croton dam is a mighty *fact*, to be admired and wondered at, while it does not stir the heart like the memorials which we left behind us at Irvington and Sleepy Hollow.

STONY POINT, three miles above Haverstraw, on the west side of the river, has a record in history. It commands the waters of the Hudson, which are here contracted into a very narrow channel.

Wayne's Black Walnut, one of our few historical trees, stood, till within a few years, on the river side of the road between Haverstraw and Stony Point.

"I'll storm hell, if you will only plan it," said the impetuous General Wayne—Mad Anthony, as his countrymen called him—when conversing with Washington on the subject of attacking the fort on Stony Point, in the summer of 1779.

At noon on the 15th of July, Wayne led a large party of Massachusetts infantry cautiously through the defiles of the mountains, and at eight o'clock in the evening rendezvoused in a thicket below the fort. He had formed his plans with care. The dogs in the neighborhood were all killed to prevent their attracting the notice of the sentinels by barking. A shrewd negro, named Pompey, furnished the officers of the garrison with berries and fruit, had their unbounded confidence, and obtained the countersign regularly on the plea that, it being hoeing-corn time, his master would not let him go to the fort except at night. He was employed by Wayne as his guide. Under a large black walnut tree, on the border of the thicket, and not far from the road, Wayne gave his orders to his officers, and directed them to follow Pompey. At eleven o'clock they moved from that tree toward the fort as stealthily as tigers crouching for their prey. Pompey gave the countersign to the sentinels, and, while conversing with them, they were seized and gagged by the Americans. Thus silence was secured and alarm prevented, until the party, in two columns, ascended the rough promontory on which the fort lay. Then they answered picket-guns by bayonet thrusts. The garrison were aroused by the cry, " To arms !" It was too late; victory was with Wayne; and at two o'clock in the morning he wrote to Washington : " Dear General, the American flag waves here." The present light-house and bell-tower marks the site of the old fort, and are always pointed out.

Opposite, on the eastern shore, is VERPLANCK'S POINT, which may be recognized from the steamer's deck, by several large brick-making establishments, with their kilns and drying-houses.

Between Stony, and Verplanck's Points the river is only half a mile in width. Upon this narrow pass look down commanding heights, and both the British foe and the rebel freemen estimated its advantages and contended for its possession in old '76.

PEEKSKILL is reached soon after rounding Verplanck's Point. We have lingered long upon our way hither, and yet have recounted but a few of the traditions of the past, or the stories of the present. We have now reached a village which will some day be made famous. The most popular of American pulpit orators, whose name is a household word through the Eastern and Northern States, has for many years resided in summer on his " place," a little east of the village. We say *place* advisedly, for although the reverend gentleman himself often writes and speaks of it as a *farm*, he also gives us such appalling accounts of the expense of raising cabbages and potatoes there, that we are constrained to believe, that if his success is a fair sample of the ordinary lot of farmers, our country will certainly be brought to financial ruin by its unlucky farming element.

STONY POINT.

By-and-by, this busy brain will work no more. The large heart will cease its beating. The faithful leader of souls will go " up higher." *Then* a history of the most gifted of the " Beecher family" will be written, which will unveil somewhat of the charms with which its central figure has invested that happy Peekskill home. *We* dare say no more. Would that Fanny Fern, who praises or criticises with the most charming and audacious disregard of " whether folks like it, or not," would pay a visit to Peekskill, and gossip about it thereafter. There's a hint for you, Fanny! Please, take it in good part, and not give us a " Ledger lecture " for venturing the suggestion.

Peekskill was, in 1797, the headquarters of "old Israel Putnam," then a commander in our army. The oak tree is still shown upon which he hung Palmer, the British spy.

The Van Cortlandt house in this vicinity is one of the old houses of which we have too few. It was once the temporary residence of Washington. Near it is a venerable church, erected in 1767, within whose churchyard stands a monument to Paulding, one of the captors of Andre.

Many a gay party rides over to Lake Mahopac from Peekskill. Lake Mahopac lies in the western part of the town of Carmel, Putnam County. The lake is nine miles in circumference, and about fourteen miles from the Hudson at Peekskill. It is an attractive Summer resort, but can never vie with the charms of Lake George, nor will Fashion ever hold here the perpetual festival of Saratoga.

Mahopac is five miles distant from Croton Falls, a station on the New York and Harlem railway. To this line we shall make few allusions, as it has grown up to meet the exigencies of travel through a region which is neither as rich in historic or modern interest as the route we have chosen.

The friends of the Tribune and its veteran editor, will not fail to criticise us, however, if we dismiss the Harlem road from notice without a mention of Chappaqua, one of its stations, near which is located the farm of Horace Greeley.

Mr. Bonner has a pleasant word for Mr. Greeley, who, he says, goes up to his farm, "Chappaqua" (or Chop-away), on Fridays, and that, on arriving, he immediately proceeds to chop. He never foregoes that. Mr. Greeley is not only very courteous in showing visitors around, but manifests great enjoyment in the scenery, and in pointing out the different sights; but, after a while, he says to his visitor: "If you will amuse yourself a while now, I guess I'll do a little chopping." Mr. Greeley has done a good deal with the axe in his day. He has lopped off many useless limbs from the political tree, hewed off any number of decayed and dead branches, tapped numberless "sap-heads," successfully set a goodly number of fruit-bearing grafts, remorselessly hacked down scores of useless old trees, and pulled out of their roots hundreds of old stumps that encumbered the earth and prevented the growth of those public crops for which Mr. G. has so long been laboring on the national farm. "Chappaqua" affords a fine illustration of what can be accomplished by industrious, intelligent farming—and plenty of capital.

In Westchester County, there is A HOME, to which we must allude.

The alarming prevalence of consumption in the vicinity of New York has induced a number of influential gentlemen to establish a "Home for Consumptives," where such relief as is possible may be afforded to those suffering with this disease. For the present, a building has been secured at Tremont, Westchester County, and all comforts suitable for patients have been provided. Medical aid of the best character will be afforded, and nothing will be left undone, which will tend to invigorate or sustain the afflicted. There are now accommodations for thirty; and, as soon as possible, land will be secured at White Plains, a station upon the Harlem line, and permanent and suitable buildings be erected. The design is to make the institution a perfectly free charity; but, in the outset, money is received from patients who have means, because the funds of the society are not ample.

Another enterprise of interest has been recently projected at New Rochelle, a delightful town in Westchester County, which is reached by the trains upon the New York and New Haven road. Something similar to the well known Llewellyn Park, of Orange, N. J., has been laid out at or near New Rochelle, and called Huguenot Park—named, we suppose, from the fact that New Rochelle was originally settled by French Huguenots.

This large enclosure is to be held in common by owners of adjacent property whose grounds open into it—all its groves, its lawns, its drives, its rocky eminences, becoming, as it were, a part of each man's premises.

This park contains five hundred acres, and includes within its limits a magnificent forest of about one hundred and fifty acres, several small lakes of great beauty, and numerous picturesque scenes. A portion of the ground is very high, and affords splendid views of the Sound, the Long Island shore, the Hudson Palisades, and a wide expanse of country, dotted with villages and farms.

It is owned by the Huguenot Park Association, comprised of numerous wealthy gentlemen in New Rochelle and vicinity. The grounds have been laid out in English landscape style; the whole has been thoroughly drained; winding drives of ample width extend for six miles through a varied succession of hill and dale, forest and lawn; and every means taste could suggest has been used to enhance the picturesque beauties of the place.

Pass on the good example, Friends, through the Empire State. It is by combined efforts of this kind that parks may be rendered abundant; and now, before it is too late, tracts of native beauty in proximity to our towns should be saved from the axe and the plough.

But we must return to the vicinity of Peekskill, and then bid farewell to this fair Westchester County.

The time is rapidly approaching when railroad trains will fly with lightning speed from one end of our continent to the other, without even stopping to "take a drink" by the way. A novel method of supplying locomotives with water, which has been in use for some time in England, is about to be introduced into our country. The Hudson River Railroad Company have already made successful experiments. At Montrose Station, near Peekskill, there was constructed, not long since, in the centre of the track, a trough, one thousand two hundred feet in length, fifteen inches in depth, and eighteen inches wide. This was lined with sheet iron, heavily painted. The trough is perfectly straight, will hold sixteen thousand gallons of water, and is fed by a couple of springs. A locomotive was also fitted up with an ingeniously constructed pipe, connecting with the tender, and having a nozzle which can be instantaneously dropped into the water, while the train is running thirty miles an hour. When the first experiment was made, the water rushed with a roar into the tender, filling it to the complete satisfaction of all concerned.

Query—will thirsty passengers ever be supplied in the same wholesale way upon "fast" trains? But there is heat, bustle and dust upon the train—silence with our stately steamer.

Above Peekskill is Anthony's Nose, a prominent *feature* of the river, rising, as it does, one thousand two hundred and twenty-eight feet. From this point to Fort Montgomery, a chain was extended in the Revolution, and some of the links are now in the Albany State Library.

A little below Anthony's Nose, upon the opposite shore, is Donderberg, or Thunder Mountain. The old legend runs, that the Dutch goblin who keeps the Donderberg, brings down frightful squalls upon such craft as fail to drop the peaks of their mainsails in salute as they pass.

CALDWELL'S LANDING lies directly opposite Peekskill, and is noted as the spot where such persistent and enthusiastic search has been vainly made for the hidden treasures of the famous Captain Kidd. Remains of the apparatus used for this purpose are still seen in bold, black relief at the Donderberg Point, as the boat rounds it toward the Horse-race.

At Peekskill, the river makes a sudden turn to the west, which is called the race, and we have fairly entered the HIGHLANDS.

IV.

NIAGARA has its majestic grandeur—Lake George its picturesque beauty—but the Hudson has West Point and the Highlands. Around West Point cluster a thousand memories and traditions; memories of the Revolution and the heroes who fought the good fight which gave us our freedom; memories which cling to the crumbling walls of old Fort Putnam, still grimly frowning above the green, smooth-cut sward of the Parade; traditions of romantic adventures and of hair-breadth escapes; traditions of the escapades of wild cadets, now grown gray in their country's service, and wearing hard-earned laurels; traditions of the cadet-life of those whose memory will ever live in the hearts of their countrymen—a better and more lasting witness of their courage, virtue and nobility, than the shafts of monumental stone raised to their memory by surviving comrades, and placed on the very spot where they, in the first flush of health and hope and opening manhood, dreamed of long, happy and noble lives.

VIEW FROM WEST POINT.

West Point has sent forth an army of gentlemen, of scholars and of warriors. It has also sent forth a band of engineers, to whose peaceful labors our mariners owe a never-ending debt of gratitude—engineers who have patiently and laboriously mapped the coast of a continent, and marked the reefs and shoals which had often wrecked the home-bound vessel, almost in sight of port.

West Point has ennobled all who have endeavored to *profit* by its advantages. There are names now tarnished, which once stood high upon its roll-call. There are those also who were very nearly the "Boobies" of their class, whose later career has been honored and brilliant.

West Point is a great centre of interest during the examinations, which are conducted in the month of June. *Then*, the family friends of the enterprising cadets, and many who secretly fancy they may sometime be the "nearer one yet and the dearer," as well as scores of butterflies who only want to have a good time somewhere, turn their faces thitherward.

West Point always looks charmingly fresh and green in leafy June. We mean nothing personal toward the cadets by this remark, and indeed need not fear that any military youth will construe it as such, for a more self-satisfied individual than the average West Point cadet is scarcely to be found anywhere in the world.

Those who are interested in military tactics and drill, will be best pleased with West Point in July and August, when the cadets go into camp, and lead the life of soldiers in the field. Drills, parades and guard-mountings are the order of the day.

At the close of August, a grand ball is given by the cadets. The next day they "break up camp," and resume their regular quarters and studies.

Cozzens' West Point Hotel commands a fine view of the Military Buildings. Upon its piazza, on a fine June afternoon, President Grant can be seen enjoying his after-dinner cigar, and so, I presume, have a majority of the Presidents before him.

This house was also for many years the summer headquarters of the late Lieutenant-General Scott, who died here in May, 1866.

It was Washington who first suggested West Point as the most eligible situation for the Military Academy. The first steps were taken by Congress to establish it in 1802, but the school was not in operation until 1812. The average number of cadets is about two hundred and fifty. The academy is of stone, two hundred and seventy-five feet long by seventy-five feet wide, and three stories high. The United States lands were purchased (two thousand one hundred and five acres), and control over two hundred and fifty acres in extent was ceded by New York to the General Government in 1826.

Kosciusko's Garden and Monument are on the river bank, near the camp-ground. Near the Garden is a fine Spring, said to have been discovered by the Patriot himself. His monument is of white marble. It was erected by the corps of cadets in 1828, at a cost of five thousand dollars.

Chain Battery Walk, which leads here from the North Wharf, has been trod by the feet of many distinguished people, as next to the Government Buildings and the parade ground. Kosciusko's Garden is one of the chief *show places* of this region.

Upon the parade ground a bronze statue of General John Sedgwick has been erected within a few years. The ruins of Forts Clinton, Putnam, Webb and Wyllys are sometimes visited.

In the river, opposite West Point, lies Constitution Island, upon which portions of the fortifications of '76 are still to be seen.

NEAR COZZENS' LANDING.

CROW NEST.

We may be pardoned, perhaps, for mentioning the more modern interest which is attached to Constitution Island, as the home of Miss Susan Warner and her sister. All book-lovers will remember the sensation created by Miss Warner's "Wide, Wide World," in 1850. Thirty-five thousand copies are said to have been sold in the United States alone.

Miss Warner's numerous writings have attained a just celebrity, though some of her books are open to the criticism, that one cannot read them without feeling guilty of eavesdropping at a parlor key-hole, where some "tall" love-making is in progress.

Her literary success enabled her to purchase her present pleasant home. It is said that the apples in her orchard look very inviting to the "boys," when they row across to the Island.

There are rumors afloat, hinting that the literary sisters have more than once rushed forth, with woman's natural weapon, the broomstick, in hand, to drive from their cherry trees an invading foe. We don't vouch for this story, mind you—but we *will* say, that perhaps it is just as well that the soil and the climate of Constitution Island are not favorable to the growth of water melons, for we should fear that a melon patch would never "do well" under the shadow of West Point.

Cozzens' Hotel, one and one-half miles below Cozzen's *West Point* Hotel, occupies a splendid situation, and is kept by a proprietor who believes in "printer's ink," and by its aid drew one hundred and sixty guests hither during the first week in June of the present year. For many years, crowds have come here in the heats of July and August—now, the Saratoga trunks arrive as early as the house is open for guests.

The Parry House nestles on the river bank, close by, and is a fine *new* hotel. On one side are the mountains, abounding in walks and horseback rides, and in magnificent views and romantic lakes that furnish occupation to the artist and the sportsman. On the other, the Hudson flows grandly by, dotted with white sails, musical with the splashing of wheels of numerous steamers, furnishing a broad, cool avenue from hot, dusty streets to the green hill-sides.

The West Shore railroad is enthusiastically prophesied by West Pointers, and we do not doubt that it will be an accomplished fact in "the good time coming." The village of Highland Falls, in this vicinity, is so rarely noted by the river tourist, that few dream of a census report for it of three thousand inhabitants as permanent population, and over four thousand in the summer season.

The Donald-Highland Institute is situated in the village of Highland Falls, half a mile from Cozzens' Hotel and Landing, and a little more than a mile below West Point Military Academy.

This school, under the charge of Robert Donald, A. M., affords superior facilities for fitting pupils to pass the West Point examinations. Parents who seek a school for their sons where *constant progress* is the aim and rule, will do well to bear in mind the Donald-Highland Institute.

During "the season," the Institute is transformed into a home for summer visitors, and becomes one of the most important of the Oak Grove cottages, under the care of Messrs. Goodsell Bros.

It is a romantic walk from Highland Falls to the Steamboat and Ferry landing. Upon the opposite shore the Hudson River trains, like jointed reptiles, glide along, pausing at Station Garrison, to acommodate travel to, and from, West Point.

Among the Highlands, on the eastern shore, opposite West Point, at an elevation of four hundred feet above the river, stands an old Episcopal church, built in 1760.

COLD SPRING.

It is said, that one of the aids of Washington, when riding by this church and noticing its windows broken in, said: "General, that is a Tory church!"

"No!" replied Washington, indignantly. "If that is a Tory church, then I am a Tory."

Two miles distant are the picturesque "Indian Falls," which have been so often seen upon canvas by those who will never discover whether in reality there are "pictures in its amber water."

COLD SPRING is two miles north of Garrison's Station, on the Hudson River railway. It is a village upon the hill-side, above which rises the stately granite crown of Bull Hill—called by classical folks, Mt. Taurus.

Upon an elevated plateau, near the village, is Undercliff, the country seat of the late George P. Morris, where for many years a princely hospitality was extended to guests from the literary and fashionable circles of the metropolis. Over this attractive home, presided Mrs. Morris, the lovely lady who furnished Washington Irving with the original of his beautiful portrait of "The Wife," in a sketch which has perhaps been as much admired as any effort of his pen.

Standing upon the terrace at Undercliff, and looking across the river, we see *old Cro' Nest* and *Storm King*. Above old Cro' Nest, on summer eves, rises the Evening Star, resting, to all appearance, as directly upon its summit as if it were placed there by human hands for an ornament or a beacon light. Sweeter words were never penned, than Morris wrote, referring to this star on Cro' Nest's brow:

"Where Hudson's wave, o'er silvery sands,
  Winds through the hills afar,
Old Cro' Nest, like a Monarch, stands,
  Crowned with a single star."

The scene of "The Culprit Fay"—Rodman Drake's exquisite poem—was laid among these hills, where

> "The Moon looks down on old Cro' Nest,
> She mellows the shade on his shaggy breast,
> And seems his huge, gray form to throw,
> In a Silver Cone on the wave below!"

The name "Crow Nest" was at first applied to a deep, rocky depression which exists near the summit, but of late years the term has been adopted for the mountain itself.

Breakneck Hill, which rises above Mt. Taurus, separated from it by a valley, formerly owned a genuine "Old Man of the Mountain." But, alas! we went to war with Mexico, and blasted some of Nature's northern fortresses to furnish rock for the construction of artificial southern forts, and the natural curiosity known as St. Anthony's face was forever destroyed. It may be said that the head is broken, but the *Neck* remains.

Near Cold Spring is the celebrated Foundry where the Parrott guns are cast.

Upon the western shore of the Hudson is CORNWALL LANDING, one of the most gay and fashionable resorts upon the river.

In the vicinity of Storm King, upon a lofty plateau, which is reached by either the Newburgh or the Cornwall road, is Idlewild. Here, with that "rose on his cheek whose root is Death," the Poet, Willis, came to die, and lived fifteen years—an invalid, whose life was prolonged by the pure atmosphere of the mountains.

NEWBURGH is one of the most delightful places upon the Hudson. It is an old town—a fashionable town—a hospitable town. Here, Washington made his headquarters during the war. Here, the last survivor of Washington's Life Guard was buried, in 1856. His monument is erected near the Old Stone House of Revolu-

WASHINGTON'S HEADQUARTERS AT NEWBURGH.

tionary fame—a view of which we present elsewhere. In this house are treasured all sorts of relics: old Hessian boots that, by their weight, were evidently never intended for those " who fight and run away"—victory or capture would inevitably be the portion of their wearers; old swords which have a history written in blood; trappings of soldiers, that have lost the glitter and the tinsel, " the pride, the pomp and circumstance of glorious war;" and a piano of such discord that rash critics might suppose it to date back to the time of the Flood rather than the Revolution.

The Old House was built in 1750, and is now the property of the State. Many of the scenes in Cooper's novel of " The Spy" were laid in this vicinity.

Newburgh was settled in 1698. It has a population of about fifteen thousand, and is the termination of the Newburgh Branch of the Erie railway, by which over a million tons of coal are annually delivered, and shipped by water to various destinations.

Lovers of the fine arts will regard the coal interests of this place as secondary to its interest as the late home of the lamented Downing, whose works upon Landscape Gardening and Horticulture have rendered his name familiar to all Americans—and also as the residence of Mr. Henry Kirke Brown, the sculptor, to whom was intrusted the commission of executing the colossal Lincoln statue in New York city, the subscriptions to which were made by dollar contributions.

The Lincoln statue is of bronze, eleven feet in height, standing on a granite pedestal twenty-two feet high. It is erected on Union Square, at the opposite angle from that occupied by the Washington equestrian statue.

It is now about fifteen years since Mr. Brown removed from the heights of Brooklyn to the picturesque banks of the Hudson. It is needless to say that, with his talent and opportunity, he has made his house and grounds all that refined taste and abundant means can accomplish. We particularly desire, however, to speak of the works of art of national importance now under his hands.

Mr. Brown is at present at work on his equestrian statue of General Scott. For more than four years he has been laboring almost uninterruptedly on the horse, and we think it will prove the greatest triumph of the kind in modern art. The model is an exact copy of the Lexington stock, made with the most minute fidelity, and yet with great spirit, from one of the best living specimens ever raised on the "Alexander farm." This bronze horse, when erected on its pedestal, will be nine and one-half feet from the forefeet to its shoulders, and about twelve feet to the ears. With General Scott astride, the group will be over sixteen feet high. The expression of the whole will be the embodiment of earnest repose, such as would inspire horse and rider at the moment when the fate of the battle pending is in a balance—the moment when theatrical display is nonsense—and we think the artist's earnest conception is thoroughly embodied, and will be appreciated by the most careless observer as by the closest student of art. This promised great work is for Washington city.

We are thankful that something truly admirable in the sculptor's art is soon to be seen at the national capital. The public will be interested in learning from an authority as good as Mr. Brown, that we have facilities in this country for casting works of art in bronze equal to any in Europe.

Apropos of another art than sculpture. We hear that one of the most remarkable feats of skating upon record was performed last winter by three " fast " young men from Newburgh. It is, at least, without parallel in the history of skating on the Hudson. In seven

THE RESIDENCE AND PLEASURE GROUNDS OF PROF. H. G. EASTMAN, of Poughkeepsie, N. Y., the President and founder of Eastman Business College.

mies, military and public schools, are among the best and most prosperous in the land. The very atmosphere is impregnated with the aroma of culture. Thousands of men and women scattered throughout our land, have hung the choicest rooms in the human temple with memory pictures selected from happily spent school hours in this beautiful city.

Prominent among these, we mention Vassar College, for the education of young women, the first institution of the kind ever attempted. This magnificent structure was founded by the late Matthew Vassar, at an expense of nearly a million of dollars, and constructed after the model of the Tuileries at Paris.

It is finely situated, amid agreeable scenery, in a high and healthful situation. All its appointments are on the most liberal scale. It has a laboratory, a museum, a library, an observatory, and all the other usual adjuncts of a well-endowed seat of learning; and has, besides, a gallery of art, containing a fine collection of water-color paintings, including four by Turner; a gymnasium and riding-school; and two hundred or more acres, laid out partly as a park, and partly cultivated as a farm.

It is told in Poughkeepsie, with some glee and pride, that a class of young ladies, having been taught surveying, when a question arose as to the boundaries of the Vassar College domain, were sent out "with the chain," and actually discovered and rectified an error, and settled the question in dispute.

Eastman's Business College is also a Poughkeepsie institution. It is undoubtedly the best of its kind in the country, and leads all other business schools in the one grand element of success—the combination of theory and practice.

In how far this institution has supplied the wants of young men, and accomplished the purposes of its President, is demonstrated by the long list of its graduates occupying responsible positions in every city of this Union, and the unsolicited testimonials of gentlemen distinguished in every walk of life.

Such has been the success of this College, that, starting ten years ago with one student, its catalogue now exhibits the unparalleled number of seventeen thousand, who have circulated not less than five millions of dollars in this city.

In addition to the above named institutions, there are nearly a score of others for the instruction of youth.

The Collingwood Opera House, an elegant Music Hall, capable of seating twenty-two hundred people, is also a source of pride to Poughkeepsie.

A Memorial Fountain has been reared in the Soldier's Park, on South avenue,

"TO THE PATRIOT DEAD OF DUTCHESS COUNTY."

This is one of the finest fountains in the United States, and is the lion of Poughkeepsie in attracting the notice and admiration of strangers.

A magnificent building is now in process of erection—the Insane Asylum—on the Hyde Park road, three miles from the city. It is intended to be one of the finest and most complete structures of its kind in the country.

There are private residences in this pleasant inland city which command views of the Hudson of unsurpassed beauty. The pleasure drives in this vicinity are also remarkably fine. We doubt whether there can be found in Europe many twelve mile drives which are more beautiful and romantic in natural scenery, or richer in splendid villas and ornamental grounds, than the six miles south on South avenue and north on the Hyde Park road.

THE SOLDIERS' MEMORIAL FOUNTAIN.
Opposite Eastman Place, Poughkeepsie, N. Y.

NEAR NEWBURGH.

hours and five minutes they skated from Newburgh to Albany, a distance of one hundred miles, notwithstanding the ice was very rough in many places.

FISHKILL LANDING, upon the east bank of the river, is the port, so to speak, of Fishkill, lying five miles in the interior. It was in the neighborhood of Fishkill that the celebrated spy, Miss Montcrieffe, pursued her avocation during the struggle for Independence. Many elegant residences of New Yorkers are here.

NEW HAMBURGH comes next, with its black and terrible record of recent railway disaster.

Between New Hamburgh and Poughkeepsie is the residence of Professor Morse, the inventor of the electric telegraph—the man through whose agency men now speak to one another, though separated by the width of the earth, with the lightning's speed, and as if standing face to face.

POUGHKEEPSIE has been often called the Central Park of the Hudson river. It occupies one of the finest, if not the finest, site of any inland city on the continent, and commands the admiration of all who visit it.

This flourishing and beautiful city, containing a population of twenty thousand, is situated on the eastern bank of the Hudson, midway between New York, the commercial, and Albany, the political centre of the State, partly on a hill sloping to the river, but chiefly on a high, level plateau, and is the centre of a highly cultivated section of the State, not surpassed by any in the Union. Its streets are numerous and spacious, are proverbial for their cleanliness—beautifully shaded, with sidewalks neatly paved. Its public buildings and private residences are constructed on a scale commensurate with the wealth, liberality and public spirit of its citizens.

In the business portions of the city, buildings which a few years since answered all the requirements of the age, are rapidly giving way to structures of a more substantial and ornamental character, approximating the palatial style of the metropolis; while in the more retired sections, and along our beautiful avenues, the city is rapidly extending its limits, many families of affluence from abroad preferring a quiet, suburban residence, with its retirement and relaxation, to the noise and the gaiety of the fashionable summer resorts. The consequence is, that real estate is rapidly appreciating in value, and on every side are witnessed substantial evidences of progress and prosperity.

Even a cursory view of the location of this city and its surroundings will distinguish it as pre-eminently healthy. Its elevation, one hundred feet above the level of the river, the purity and dryness of the atmosphere, the scrupulous cleanliness of its streets— all conspire to make it one of the healthiest cities in the world. Innumerable instances might be given of the salutary effect of this climate on strangers affected with pulmonary and rheumatic affections, to whom a residence here has been recommended by the most eminent physicians of the country. The hotels and boarding-houses have been largely patronized for years by those who come here for relief. It is well known that this city and county, especially in the vicinity of Washington Hollow, is becoming as celebrated as Aiken, S. C.; and many wealthy gentlemen, who are obliged, on account of bronchial affection, to leave New York city, have purchased estates here.

Poughkeepsie is very proud, as she has a right to be, of her educational and literary institutions, possessing, as she does, the finest College for women, and the most practical Business College for young men, in the world; while her twenty seminaries, acade-

In justice to the city, we must add, that " mine host " of the Morgan House knows " how to run a hotel," and a good one, too.

There is probably no private residence on the Hudson that attracts more attention, or whose beautiful grounds are more admired, than the one we illustrate here—the home of Mayor Eastman, of Poughkeepsie. Not only so on account of their location—twenty-seven acres, situated almost in the very heart of the city, where property is reckoned by the foot—and the expense incurred and taste displayed in buildings and grounds, but because the entire place has been open to citizens and strangers alike to drive in, and walk in, since the first day Professor Eastman became the possessor of the property.

The wall that encloses it is one of the finest and most expensive fences that encloses any private grounds in this country. We give a view of the marble entrance, and also one looking south. This wall is coped with white marble, and the circular entrance is composed of solid white marble piers. On the street side it is built low so as to give the passer-by a delightful view of the fine lawns and grounds. No gates are visible on the place, but broad, open entrances, inviting you to walk in and share the enjoyment with the proprietor.

The garden and grounds are well stocked with choice flowers, shrubs, and trees of all kinds, and more are added yearly.

The residence is a large building, with towers, verandas, Mansard roof, and richly ornamented. The style of architecture is peculiar, but displays admirable taste. The interior of this house is decidedly original, and a model of convenience.

Nothing adds more to the beauty of pleasure grounds than a well-kept, closely-cut lawn. The lawn on this place is a model indeed, and is the pride of the proprietor and the city, as it may well be, for we doubt if a more beautiful and perfect piece of greensward was ever laid down than this. It is not only admired by citizens, who may be found in large numbers any pleasant day looking on it from the terraced walks, but by many from surrounding towns, who drive in to admire it, and also by strangers, who come from a distance to enquire how such perfection in lawn making can be accomplished.

In the center of the grounds, and in full view of the main street, is a circular drive of a quarter of a mile in circumference, twenty-two feet wide, lined with trees on either side. A neat fence on the inside of this circle encloses a Deer Park of four acres, which is stocked with deer, swan, and fancy birds.

In this park is a large pond, with an island in the center, from which several fountains are constantly playing. The scene, looking down on this part of the ground from the street above, with the circular road, the dark, green lawn, the graceful deer and birds, the fine terraced banks, the grounds of the Skating Park in the distance, with the fine building of the Riverview Military School in the background, is one of great beauty, and is enjoyed daily by many.

The Eastman College Band frequently give concerts on the lawn, where we have seen from three to five thousand people present, and on any pleasant Sunday afternoon, South avenue is thronged with those strolling past these grounds. Professor Eastman, also, generously throws them open to societies and organizations visiting the city, and the military of Albany, the firemen of New York, Philadelphia, and other places, remember his hospitalities with gratitude.

The illustrations which we give of these grounds will be admired by all lovers of the beautiful.

VIEW ON THE GROUNDS OF EASTMAN PLACE, POUGHKEEPSIE, N. Y
Showing the Terrace Block of Elegant Modern Residences, now being erected by Prof. EASTMAN.

We have presented here a picture which has much *sunlight* upon it. Let us add to it one shadow—relating a life history, in which "truth seems stranger than fiction."

The death of "Lochy Ostrom," some two years ago, at the age of seventy-seven, unveiled a sad story.

For years she had been, to all outward appearance, a cold-hearted, calculating, avaricious woman; and investigations after her death, disclosed property hid away in an old trunk under her bed, to the value of over twenty-one thousand five hundred dollars, besides papers showing that she owned real estate to the value of twelve thousand dollars. But other things, more romantic than bonds, or gold and silver, were also found. A bundle of love-letters, seventeen in all, was tied neatly with a piece of white satin ribbon, but the ribbon was stained with time, and the paper on which the letters were written was also stained. In one of the bedrooms, although Lochy was known not to have bought two dresses in ten years, were found twenty dresses, four or five of which were of elegant and costly silk, apparently at least fifty years old. Visible, also, were pots of preserves, canned fruits, etc. Far back on the shelf was found a shriveled, dried-up fruit cake. It looked as if it had been there threescore years. It was highly ornamented, and on the top, in the center, was a sugar Cupid. It was very carefully stowed away. The letters revealed her secret history. In her young days " Lochy " had a lover who was devotedly attached to her, and she loved him in return. The match was broken off by her parents, and the disappointed suitor moved away from the place to Cincinnati. Twice he journeyed back to again offer her his heart and hand; but she fancied her duty to her parents forbade her acceptance. The lover seems to have appreciated her filial love, yet to have felt that if her love for him had been entire, she would have accepted his proposal, in which the mother whom she cared for, was not forgotten. He married another woman, who died after a few years. He kept up his correspondence with "Lochy" at long intervals; but she had become hard and cold. Thirty-five or forty years after the commencement of their acquaintance he again made an offer of marriage; but she was gray and wrinkled, with all affection gone, save for her money. She refused the offer, and neither saw nor heard again from him who had been her lover. Such is real life.

Several quiet places above Poughkeepsie nestle amid the hills on either bank of the Hudson.

Ice and apples are largely exported from this vicinity. The famous apple farm of R. L. Pell, Esq., is upon the west side of the river, with its twenty-five thousand apple-trees. Opposite, and about one mile above Hyde Park landing, is "Placentia," the home of the late honored writer, James K. Paulding, the friend of Washington Irving.

Upon the west bank of the river is the summer residence of John Astor, Esq. Esopus Island lies in the river, where the steamer Berkshire was burned in 1864.

RHINEBECK has many interesting residences and old traditions. Its bears gold in its bosom, and we predict that a "gold fever" will some day make the old town famous.

Wildercliff is here, a country seat built by the late Freeborn Garretson, an eminent preacher whose name is identified with the annals of the Methodist Episcopal Church. The place may be recognized by its broad lawn, which lies in front of the house.

Ellerslie, the home of the Hon. William Kelly, is a large estate of over six hundred acres. Guests may walk for several miles amid his ornamented grounds.

EASTMAN PLACE, POUGHKEEPSIE, N. Y.
The Walk on South Avenue

A little above Rhinebeck is Rokeby, owned, and occupied in summer, by William B. Astor. It is distinguished to the eye of the Tourist by its tower and pointed roof.

Above Rokeby is Montgomery Place. This is a domain of surpassing beauty. The house was built by the widowed Bride of General Montgomery, who met his untimely fate at Quebec in 1775. After fifty years of widowhood, Mrs. Montgomery was succeeded, in her ownership of the place, by her brother, Mr. Edward Livingston, whose family still occupy it.

Upon the eastern bank of the river, one mile below Catskill Landing and five miles from the city of Hudson, is Clermont, which in the last century was the great *show place* upon the Hudson. Here stood the original Livingston Manor. Here Chancellor Livingston resided, and built also an elegant home for his mother. He paid a heavy penalty for patriotism when both the houses were burned during the Revolution; but new houses have since been erected, and Claremont is still a splendid country seat.

The Hudson may well be called the "steamboat river," and it should not be forgotten that the success of Robert Fulton was largely due to the hearty co-operation and the gold of the Chancellor. Indeed, Mr. Livingston projected the plan of a steam vessel before Fulton's genius had incepted the stirring idea which resulted in that steamboat *named Claremont*, christened by the people "Fulton's Folly," in which the ascent of the Hudson was fairly accomplished in September, 1809, just two hundred years later than Hendrick Hudson's voyage of discovery.

Mr. Livingston's friendship availed to secure for Fulton, fame in his lifetime, and a place of rest in the Livingston vault of Trinity churchyard, when for Fulton the honors of earth were as "low as graves brought down."

The estate of Clermont extends some twelve miles along the Hudson. The finest specimens of the Yellow Locust to be found in this country adorn this place—one of them measuring sixteen feet in circumference.

A little above Poughkeepsie the river bends, and the finest point is gained. It is a foreground of cultivated and foliaged hills of great variety of outline, rising as they recede, and ranging and towering at last along the horizon, in the Catskill mountains. These are the "ever-changing, legendary Kaatsbergs." When the red men ruled, they were called Onti Ora, or the Mountains of the Sky. When the white man first reared his rude home in the wilderness, the panther's scream rang so often and so drearily in his ear, that, in scornful impatience and old-fashioned Dutch, he named them Kaats-bergs, or Cat Mountains.

The Catskills have always been dear to the heart of the Geologist, for here are the exposed strata of all the principal rocks known as the New York system. From the vicinity of these mountains, paving stones are transported to New York city.

Above Catskill village, an immense ice-house has been recently built.

There is never a stir in this place. Quiet contentment seems to be the rule of life.

A new hotel, the Irving House, has been recently erected, and is just open for the accommodation of the public. Those who seek the comforts of fine, airy rooms, newly and nicely furnished—a good table and good attendance—will not be disappointed here.

Many pleasant residences overlook the long rambling village street, one of them was for many years the home, and contains the studio of Thomas Cole, the painter whose name and fame will be

forever identified with "The Voyage of Life." He was one of those to whom the free mountain air gives inspiration. At twenty-four years of age it was said of him, that his "fame spread like fire."

Among the works of his pencil his "Lake with Dead Trees," and "Falls of the Cauterskill," have greatly contributed to ensure his reputation.

His devoted widow still resides here. She regards his deserted studio as a sacred place, and no stranger's foot is permitted to cross its threshold. It is a ride of eight miles from the village to the mountains. The road is very firmly built, and is fortunate in its material of a slaty rock, and in the luxuriance of foliage, for the tangled tree-roots hold the soil together. The path climbs at first in easy zigzags, and presently pushes straight on through the woods.

Finally that nook in the mountain is reached, where nestles the Rip Van Winkle cottage. It stands within the amphitheatre, inclosed by lofty heights, reputed to be the place where the ghostly ninepin players of the mountains once held their revels, and where Rip laid down for his protracted snooze.

A magnificent panorama of nature lies before the eye as one presses onward, but the genuine Alpine traveler says "the views are graceful and generous, but not sublime. Your true mountaineer shrugs his shoulders at the shoulder of mountains which soar thousands of feet above him and are still shaggy with forest. For *him* there is no mountain sublimity save in the presence of lonely snow-peaks."

Thus we read of the Catskills, but when *we* behold for ourselves, the purple and sunset glories fade, and see the solemn shadows which the Kaatsbergs cast at nightfall, and especially when we shiver upon a feather bed at night in July, we are content to accept the Catskills as *mountains*.

The Kaaterskill or High Falls, are two miles west of the Mountain House, which is perched like an eagle's nest upon the precipice. Although the Mountain House is far below the highest summits of the range, yet portions of four States of the Union and an area of more than ten thousand miles are presented to the eye of one who sits at ease upon its breezy piazza. Still more superb views are to be had from the peaks of South Mountain and North Mountain.

When the Cauterskill Falls are seen to the best advantage, *words which command no colors* must fail to portray the rare and exquisite effect produced by the flashing water, the rich, serious green of the foliage, and the movements of the fleecy clouds, which tremble in the sky above.

Wherefore do we linger at the Falls? Many who have been there can sketch them more effectually than we. Many who have *not*, will weary of any description we can give.

A friend, who visited the Catskill Mountains not long ago, related to us the following characteristic incident, which came under his personal observation :

While the stage-coach was slowly wending its way up toward the Mountain House, one of the inside passengers—a young man whose general appearance indicated that he *should* have known the usages of good society—lighted a cigar, and began to smoke.

" You are not going to smoke *here*, with ladies inside ?" demanded a gentleman.

" Well, yes," responded the youth, languidly ; " I generally smoke whenever I get a chance." And he continued puffing.

Presently the gentleman who had spoken, called for the driver to stop. "Now, young man," said he, "I'll give you just one minute to get out!"

The youthful smoker looked his opponent in the eye, saw he had found his match, and silently got out and climbed to an outside seat.

Next morning, the gentleman met the young man on the piazza of the hotel, and, after pleasantly saluting him, remarked: "I see, from the book, that you are from Philadelphia."

"Yes, sir," responded the youth, evidently desirous the interview of the previous evening should not be recalled.

"And do you expect to go to New York on your way back?"

"Yes, sir," again was the reply.

"Well, young man," continued the gentleman, "from what I have seen of you, I think you will get into trouble in New York, and you may like to call upon me; so I will give you my card." Whereupon he handed him a bit of pasteboard, on which was the name of John A. Kennedy, Superintendent of the Metropolitan Board of Police!

Possibly he profited by the lesson.

HUDSON, one hundred and fifteen miles from New York, is a pleasant, rural city. It is built upon the slope of Prospect Hill, which rises to a height of two hundred feet. Hudson *once* threatened to out-rival Albany. It is an old place, and noted for its highly cultivated and refined society.

The Worth House is decidedly the best hotel in the place. It is a fine, commodious house, where summer travelers can pass a little time very pleasantly.

Columbia Springs, five miles from Hudson, affords a delightful drive, and is a summer resort of some note, for invalids.

A trip to Claverack Falls makes another excursion of interest— the falls have a clear leap of over ninety feet.

NEW LEBANON SPRINGS may be easily reached from Hudson. The route thither from Hudson is by the Hudson and Boston road to Chatham, and there change cars. The water at New Lebanon Springs lacks the *character* which pertains to the varied waters of Saratoga. It may be in many respects equally sanitary, but it is tasteless and inodorous.

The Shaker Village has given to Lebanon its fame. It is a unique pleasure, and quite a treat, to visit the Herbery, where the Shaker herbs are prepared; but a trip to Lebanon will hardly induce the visitant to adopt the "yea" and "nay"—the grotesque attire and whirling religious services of the Shaker band.

STUYVESANT, formerly known as Kinderhook Landing, is ten miles north of Hudson. Kinderhook, five miles east of the Landing, was the birthplace of our eighth president, Martin Van Buren. His estate of "Lindenwald," where he passed his closing years of life, is situated two miles south of the village.

The records of the old towns upon the Hudson's banks will never be fully written. Irving pencilled notes which commingled fact, fiction, and pure humor. The real and passionate stories of life in these old peculiar places have never been put in print. Newspaper reporters give publicity to bare facts once in a while—the rise, progress and ending of village comedies and tragedies, is seldom arrived at. Perhaps it is as well. Yet ere leaving this region of country, so rich in tradition and history, we cannot refrain from saying that there is a wide field for the novelist, which is as

THE HUDSON, SIX MILES BELOW ALBANY.

yet untrodden, in the annals of the North river towns. To justify our assertion we will relate one only, of the numerous stories which have been told in our hearing, in hushed tones, by winter evening fires. In Kinderhook, in the last century, a beautiful girl married in defiance of her parents' wishes. Her run-away match created quite a stir in those primitive days. Her lover was a wealthy farmer, haughty and handsome, and a man of overbearing temper. No blessing followed their union. Imperious commands on his part; quick retorts and bitter words on hers, rendered their lives miserable. Again and again the wife resolved to return that " soft answer which turneth away wrath," or to keep silence. As often as she made this vow it was broken. At last, when she was the mother of ten children, some of whom were grown up men, the unhappy woman, not in passion but in despair, with a sharp knife cut off the tip of that unruly member, *her tongue.* The wound healed in time, but speech was rendered difficult and incoherent. She passed the remainder of her days in almost utter silence.

Release came to her at last. Her divorce from a husband whom she had long ceased to love was about to be rendered in that silent chamber where death held his grim assize. A smile lit up the countenance of the dying woman. It was such a smile as belongs "to them that triumph." Her daughter drew near and asked—" what cheers you, mother?"

With difficulty came the answer—" *The tongue can no man tame! I tamed it. I meant no wrong, but to make home happier. Lord forgive me, if I sinned!*" These were her last utterances.

There is a stern, heroic pathos in such a life. Let us judge her not, that *we* be not judged!

ENIGMA.

BY S. S. COLT.

A city breaks upon my sight—
  Six letters doth its name compose—
Its domes gleam bright in the morning light,
  And at its feet a river flows!

Within a church I saw one stand,
  Wearing a priestly robe he came;
Mention *his dress*, at my command,
  You have three letters of my name!

Before him kneel a groom and bride;
  He asks: "Wilt love till life is past,
Let wealth or pinching want betide?"
  The answer is, my first and last!

My third, fourth, fifth, a word combine
  Which is by a father spoken;
And the bridegroom must his bride resign,
  And the maiden's heart is broken!

ANSWER.

Dost ask for the city I mean,
  Where lovers meet crosses and woe?
Hard matter to find it, I ween;
  Harder to find where it is not so!

In linen raiment, fair and white,
  The priest performs official rites,
By name an ALB appears in sight,
  As he, two hearts in one unites.

"Wilt have this maiden for thy wife,
  To cheer and guard when danger's nigh,
And fondly cherish all thy life?"
  Clearly the answer rings out, "AY!"

The angry father comes with speed,
  And sternly stays the nuptial rite;
To moans and tears he gives no heed,
  But nulls the BAN by parent's right!

My city she sits on a hill,
  Fairer and richer than many;
Ancient yet beautiful still,
  Our grave and stately ALBANY!

ALBANY, N. Y., *June* 15, 1871.

ALBANY.

THE CAPITAL CITY.

V.

THE oldest city in the United States, excepting St. Augustine, is Albany. As such, it claims the reverence, not only of every true-hearted Dutch-man, but of every member of the universal Yankee nation, which has no geographical limit this side of Saturn's rings. Until within a few years, Albany was, in every sense of the word, an old-fashioned town. The *Present* is still linked with the *Past* more inseparably here than in any other city in the State. To write of Albany, and disregard that conservative element which once admitted outsiders to a position in " good society," under this protest—

> "Take, take the Yankees in,
> And end this fuss,
> Or be assured, my Lords,
> They'll take in us!"

would be to present but a dry narrative of dates and directory of Public Buildings.

A *live* description of Albany will not represent it as *wholly* " a live town," according to the general American acceptation of that phrase in this present year of 1871.

And yet, with much conservatism, there is also stability and rectitude and the best representatives of the old Dutch aristocracy of long ago, are the most genial and high-toned—in all senses of the word, are among the best Men of To-Day.

A friendship formed in Albany, is a friendship for life.

A business is more slowly established here than in many places which boast of "more enterprise," but it is for this very reason more *surely* established. A house reared here is less liable than elsewhere to be swept away by the tides of progress, unless indeed it is built upon North Pearl, where the rush of business is entirely changing the character of this old and stately street. The first glimpse of Albany reminds the European traveler of some of the cities of the old world. Its spires and domes indeed

> "Gleam bright
> In morning's light."

The Delavan House and the Capitol seem to be the two head-centers of the city. The former is under the control of Mr. Charles Leland and is very well managed. The latter, it is sometimes hinted, is under the control of the highest bidder, and is *not* always well managed for the public good.

Leaving the Delavan House for a stroll over the city we will follow Broadway to State street.

Broadway was first known as Handelaer, and subsequently as Market street. State street was originally Yonkers. At the intersection of Broadway and State street stood the old Dutch Church which was torn down in 1806.

Passing up State street we see the Capitol beautifully located on Eagle street, facing State, one hundred and thirty feet above the Hudson. In front is a park of three acres, inclosed by an iron

THE FAMOUS OLD DUTCH CHURCH OF ALBANY.
Erected 1715. Demolished 1806.

fence and planted with ornamental shade trees. The present building was begun in 1803 and finished in 1807, at a cost exceeding one hundred and twenty thousand dollars. It is built of stone, faced with Nyack red freestone, ninety feet broad, fifty feet high, and was originally one hundred and fifteen feet long. In 1854, fifteen feet were added to the west end. The eastern front has an Ionic portico, with four columns of Berkshire marble, each three feet eight inches in diameter, and thirty-three feet high. The entrance hall is forty by fifty feet, and sixteen feet high, the ceiling of which is supported by a double row of reeded columns, and the floor is vaulted and laid with squares of Italian marble. Upon the north side of the hall are the office of the Adjutant-General and the Assembly Library, and on the south side the Executive Chambers. The inner Executive Chamber has a full sized portrait of General LaFayette, painted when he was in the city in 1825. The remainder of the first story is devoted to the Assembly Chamber. Upon the east side is a gallery, supported by iron pillars, for spectators. The ceiling is richly ornamented in stucco. Over the Speaker's seat is a full length portrait of Washington. In the second story, over the entrance hall, is the Senate Chamber, which contains the portraits of Governor Clinton and Columbus. Over the Assembly lobbies is the room of the Court of Appeals. The Court room contains portraits of Chancellors Lansing, Sandford, Jones and Walworth, Chief Justice Spencer, Abraham Van Vechten and Daniel Cady.

The roof of the State House is pyramidal, supporting a dome. Upon the dome stands a wooden statue of Themis, eleven feet high, holding in her right hand a sword and in her left a balance. The Senate and Assembly begin their sessions on the first Tuesday of January of each year, remaining in session one hundred days.

Visitors are admitted to Senate and Assembly Chambers only during sessions of the Legislature.

But this is not the Capitol, which *is to be*.

The new State House has been designed in the *Renaissance* style, similar to that of the Louvre in Paris, and many of the finest modern public buildings in Europe.

The location is a very commanding one, the grounds being about one hundred and seventy feet above the level of the Hudson. The main tower of this building will reach a height of three hundred feet above the street. From its cupola the valley of the Hudson, for more than thirty miles north and south, and of the Mohawk for nearly the same distance west, will be seen, as well as the intervening slopes and plains, for a circuit of more than twenty miles radius.

The open public grounds around the Capitol will have an area of ten acres, and when the building is completed, the old Capitol Library, Governor's mansion, and Congress Hall will all be removed, leaving a park on the east front of four hundred and fifty feet long and three hundred and twenty feet wide, the ornamentation of which will be made to conform to that of the structure.

That noble avenue, State street, will continue this open space for nearly half a mile eastward to the river; on the north will be Washington avenue, one hundred feet wide; on the south the continuation of State street; and on the west Swan street. All of the streets which formerly crossed this large area are now closed by law. Thus, standing upon almost the highest ground in the city, with the land falling off in all directions, except to the west, surrounded by these wide, open parks and broad avenues, with its high walls and still higher pavilions, turrets, and towers, this building will appear to great advantage.

The exterior walls are two hundred and eighty feet long north and south, and three hundred and eighty feet east and west. There are four entrances; three of which will be carriage entrances.

The main entrance will be at the east front, and will be approached by a very broad flight of steps in front up to the level of a broad terrace, which will extend across the whole east front. From this terrace will extend another broad flight of steps to the level of the first floor, and will open to a large vestibule, from which will extend broad corridors to all parts of the building. On the left of this entrance will be placed the suite of rooms designed for the use of the Governor, of his secretaries, and of the Military Department; and on the right will be rooms for two or more of the State officers, with whom the Governor has the most immediate official relations.

On the second, or principal floor, will be placed the Senate and Assembly chambers, and the State Library, all of which (in elevation) will occupy two stories, making forty-five feet of height. Rooms for the Committees, and other purposes, will also be placed upon this floor.

The Senate Chamber will be seventy-five by fifty-five feet on the floor, with a gallery on three sides, of twenty feet more width. The Assembly Chamber will be ninety-two by seventy-five feet on the floor, surrounded by a similar gallery, which in both chambers largely increases the areas of the upper portion. The Library will occupy the whole of the east front of these two stories, and will be two hundred and eighty-three feet long and fifty-four feet wide. This will be the most attractive room in the building, and perhaps in the world. Its large area and lofty proportions, its views toward the north, east and south, overlooking the city, and bringing in the valley of the Hudson and its western slopes for miles in each direction, will make it a favorite place of resort at all seasons of the year, even with those who have no taste for the mental pleasures afforded by its five hundred thousand volumes.

The great tower is sixty-six feet square, and the upper portion will be a quadrangular dome of nearly one hundred feet high, surmounted by an observatory, access to which will be had by a spiral staircase.

In the middle of the building will be an open court of one hundred and thirty by ninety feet, to give light and air to the inside rooms. This court will be a grand and attractive feature, being treated in the same elaborate manner as the exterior fronts, and will no doubt ultimately have its fountains and be surrounded with statuary.

The plans of the foundations have been prepared with great care. The entire structure will weigh one hundred and fifty thousand tons; but the great inequalities in the heights of the various walls, and the distribution of the enormously heavy fire-proof floors, and roofs sometimes laden with deep snows, bring very unequal weights upon the parts of the foundation adjacent to each other, and without this great care they would settle unequally and crack the walls, as is so frequently seen in modern private, and even in many of our public buildings.

The stone foundation of the walls commences on concrete, and is made of large blocks of close-cut limestone of from two to six tons weight, laid in regular courses, the first one of nearly the width of the concrete, and each successive one narrowed by offsets, until the wall is contracted to the width necessary to support the structure, arranged so that they will afford an equal bearing on each side of the line of the center of gravity of the walls and the weights which they are to sustain.

The work has been carried on with very rapid progress. Several hundred masons, stone-cutters, and laborers have been employed at the building, and several thousand men at the various quarries and in transportation.

All of the stone and the other materials which have come in by railway or water have been unloaded by steam-derricks, and hauled up the hill on the railway, on cars specially built for the purpose.

The building is estimated to cost four million of dollars, exclusive of the cost of the land and any additional decoration or ornamentation which may be hereafter ordered by the Legislature. It will require three more seasons to fully complete it.

The Corner Stone of the new Capitol was laid on Saturday, June 24, 1871—a day long to be remembered for its imposing ceremonies and its pitiless rain. Arrangements had been made to present an unequaled and brilliant display on this occasion. Late on the preceding Friday evening, the spirits of those having charge of the ceremonies were depressed by a bulletin from Professor Hough, of Dudley Observatory, predicting a severe storm on Saturday. But the stars were shining brightly—not a cloud could be seen. The Professor's opinions had always been considered reliable and correct; but, for this once, the anxious managers of the grand entertainment doubted the Professor's judgment. How could it possibly rain Saturday, when at midnight Friday it was as clear and pleasant as could be desired? It was, therefore, decided that the Professor was wrong. That he was not in error, can be attested *now* by thousands who were drenched upon the grand occasion.

During Friday night, and the early hours Saturday morning, thousands of strangers arrived in Albany from every section, and there were more Masons in the city than had ever been congregated together in this State. Had the weather been pleasant, there would have been not less than six thousand members of the ancient fraternity in line, and the procession would have been at least five miles long. As it was, in the drenching, soaking storm, the procession was certainly extraordinary. The military escort was in the highest degree creditable to officers and men, who, at the close of the march, were as thoroughly wet as if they had been in the river. General Woodhall and his guests, Major-General Carr and staff, rode at the head of the column, with an appearance of entire unconcern as to the weather. In fact, the General commanding marched the column over the entire route laid out by him, and added a little to it, to satisfy the people that he and his guests and his men didn't care for the rain. As they were soaked before they had been in the line ten minutes, this did not matter much.

The Burgesses and Jackson Corps were out in full strength.

The Knights Templar were excused from parade, and thus the procession was deprived of what would have been, under the circumstances, its most attractive feature. Probably not one-tenth of the Masons in the city appeared in line, and yet their numbers astonished our citizens and the many strangers who thronged the principal streets. When the procession passed up State street, the scene presented was exceedingly novel. The entire street seemed to be covered with umbrellas, and as those carrying them were pretty well covered up, scarcely a head could be seen.

At the Capitol, the ceremony of formally laying the Corner Stone was conducted according to the following Order of Proceedings:

I.

Music by Sullivan's Band.

II.

Introductory Address by Hamilton Harris, Chairman of the Board of New Capitol Commissioners.

III.

Prayer by the Rev. Dr. Ebenezer Halley.

IV.

Reading by William A. Rice, Secretary of the Board, a list of historical documents and memorials to be placed in the Corner Stone.

V.

Address by His Excellency John T. Hoffman, Governor of the State.

VI.

Depositing of the Box containing the articles for preservation in the Corner Stone, by the Governor.

VII.

Music by the Band.

VIII.

The Ceremonies of laying the Corner Stone by the Grand Lodge of Freemasons of New York, M. W. John H. Anthon, Grand Master.

IX.

Benediction.

The historical documents, newspapers, coins and et cetera, usually deposited upon similar occasions, were inclosed in a metallic Box, and deposited in the Corner Stone. Governor Hoffman's speech, which followed this ceremony, was brilliant and interesting. It was a speech worthy of the occasion and the Governor of the Empire State.

At the close of the Governor's address, the Corner Stone of the new Capital was " found square, level and plumb, true and trusty, and was laid according to the old customs by the Grand Master of Masons."

ODE

ON THE LAYING OF THE CORNER STONE, SUNG JUNE 24, 1871.

Tune—"*Sparkling and Bright.*"

From the noble rest of our Mountain crests,
    From the forests grand and hoary.
From the rivers, bright in their liquid light,
    We come in the summer's glory.
With hearts so fraught with the swelling thought
    Of the crowns our Age is wearing.
We stand in hope on the century's slope,
    A loftier labor daring.

CHORUS.

The Future hears thro' listening years,
    In chorus loud and lusty—
Our royal dome, our patriot home,
    Well formed, and true and trusty.

Our storied Past was proudly cast
    To this high and holy keeping,
And gladly lay on its stone to-day
    The fairest sheaves we're reaping.
So the record true that the Old State knew,
    Her lives of brave endeavor,
Shall stand secure while its walls endure,
    The Corner Stone forever!

CHORUS.—The Future hears, etc.

May the marble white prove a symbol bright
    Of whiter deeds unfolding,
While stronger far than her pillars are,
    The nation's life is moulding.
So its towers shall glow in their sculptured snow,
    Our happy hills adorning,
Till the workmen wait by the Temple's Gate,
    Beyond the Golden Morning.

CHORUS.—The Future hears, etc.

Among the minor details of the history of the day—next to the demand for umbrellas—we must mention the interest felt in a veteran who witnessed the laying of the corner stone of the old Capitol.

Says the Albany Evening Journal of June twenty-fourth: The reportorial question—Did you ever know a New York Capitol corner stone to be laid on such an unpleasant day as this? might seem one to which none could be found to respond pro or con. But "nothing is impossible to him that wills," according to Emerson, and " our own reporter" willed that he should have an interview with a party who could contrast this day of June, 1871, with that day of April, 1806, when the corner stone of the old Capitol was laid. Going into the Marshal's room at Martin's Hall about nine o'clock, we were introduced to an aged man with bright blue eye, Mr. James Gilbert, at your service, who would be happy to speak with you about the old days, on one of which he saw the corner stone of the old Capitol laid. Mr. Gilbert was born in October, 1782, and was a young fellow of twenty-four on the interesting occasion referred to. As he spoke to us this morning of the event, and of the gathering, "all of which he saw and a part of which he was," we felt like addressing him in the words of Webster: "Venerable man, you have come down to us from a former generation." The old gentleman's remembrance of the day was slight, but he recalls the immense gathering that surrounded Philip Van Rensselaer, who had the honor of laying the stone. He remembers that the ceremonies took place in the afternoon, and to the best of his knowledge and belief, the sun was shining brightly all day.

He also recollected that Mr. Barbour's Register in those days— that energetic Albany paper—had not a word to say in relation to the corner stone doings of 1806. He also had reminiscences of the laying of the corner stone of St. Peter's church, and other matters of ancient history.

Notwithstanding his great age and a lameness which results from the loss of a part of one of his feet by a railway accident some years ago, Mr. Gilbert still enjoys good health and is quite active and alert. Marshal Waterman very properly made provision for the old man, who was awarded an honorable place in the procession in an elegant carriage.

To return from chat which concerns our *future* Capitol, we will leave the State House to visit State Hall which is located on Eagle street, fronting Academy Park, and is considered one of the architectural ornaments of the city. It is built of white cut stone, with a colonnade in front, supported by six ionic columns, and is surmounted by a dome. It was completed in 1842, at a cost of three hundred and fifty thousand dollars. It contains the offices of the Secretary of State, Comptroller, Treasurer, Auditor of Canal Department, State Engineer, Clerk of Court of Appeals, Superintendent of Public Instruction, and Attorney-General and State Sealer of Weights and Measures. Open to visitors during business hours.

The City Hall, situated on Eagle street fronting Washington avenue, is a fine Grecian structure of white Sing Sing marble, built at a cost of about ninety thousand dollars. In front it has a recessed porch supported by six ionic columns. In the center of the hall in the second story is a statue of Hamilton, and in the common council room are portraits of the ex-Governors of the State. It is open to visitors during business hours. The Jail is located in rear of the City Hall, on Maiden lane.

The State Library is a place of much interest. It partakes to a considerable extent of the character of a museum. There are here, collections of coins, many of them presented to the State by Napoleon III; medals and engravings; the September Emancipation Proclamation of the lamented Lincoln, in his own handwriting; the original papers which Major Andre was carrying in his boot from Arnold to General Clinton; and the manuscripts of Sir Wm. Johnson and Governor Clinton, in about twenty folio volumes each.

The General Library in the upper story, with its cosy sofas and courteous attendants, and its portraits of old Governors of the State, is the most interesting room to visitors. It now contains about sixty thousand volumes. The Library building adjoins the Capitol and is a fire-proof structure, lighted with one hundred and eighty gas burners, and capable of accommodating one hundred thousand volumes. The Law Library of twenty thousand volumes, upon the lower floor, must be a paradise for lawyers—or the reverse—for it includes the laws and documents of every State in the Union. The Library is free to the public, and ladies as well as gentlemen avail themselves of its privileges.

The Hall of Military Records surpasses in interest the State Library as much as a living Tableau-Vivant transcends a copperplate engraving.

The building is of unpretending style, located at 219 State street. The Revolution; the war of 1812; the Mexican war; and the late Rebellion, have alike contributed to fill this hall, as well as to fill the pages of history. No other city in the Union can show a collection of equal value.

The most deeply interesting objects, perhaps, are the regimental flags which have been carried by our brave volunteers upon so many bloody battle fields during the late rebellion. There are also deposited many emblems of various kinds captured from the rebels by New York regiments. Inscribed on the banners are the names of the battles in which the regiments were engaged. Upon some of them we have counted seventy different inscriptions. The mere mention of the variety of objects of interest to be seen here would fill a volume. The little two-storied building is crowded with its riches.

The Bureau is opened daily—excepting Sundays—free to all —from 9 A. M. till 5 P. M.

The names of nearly thirty thousand visitors were registered here last year.

The State Arsenal is not far distant, upon Eagle street.

The State Museum of Natural History occupies a building upon State street, erected upon the site of the " Old State Hall." The collections of the Geological Survey of the State were deposited in the " Old State Hall," at the close of the field-work, in 1841-2, and their arrangement completed in 1843. The new building was erected in 1856, and occupied in 1857. The collections of Natural History occupy the main building, with the exception of the offices of the State Agricultural Society and of the Museum. The Agricultural Museum occupies the south wing of the building.

The collections are presented to the visitor in the following order: In the entrance hall there are arranged on each side a series of the building stones of New York and adjacent States, principally in blocks of a cubic foot, and variously dressed on the different faces, having one side presenting the natural fractured surface. These blocks consist of granites, sandstones or freestones, marbles, limestones, etc., with some polished slabs of marble.

The first floor of the Museum is devoted to the Geological and Palæontological collections. The Geological collection contains representative specimens of every rock formation; each group or division occupying a division of the table cases which extend in regular order, from the oldest formation at the beginning of the series, around the room and terminating with cases containing specimens of the superficial formations, as clay, sand, gravel, boulders, marl, tufa, peat, etc. This arrangement affords a simple and easy guide to the study of the successive formations. There are likewise a corresponding series of wall cases with more numerous or larger specimens of the same formations as those of the table cases.

The Palæontological collection is arranged in table cases upon the same floor. Beginning near the entrance of the room, a printed card of directions attached to the first case indicates that the collection is arranged in strict geological or chronological order, commencing with the oldest fossiliferous rock, and reading thence to the right the successive formations are arranged in their order. Under each of the rock formations or groups, the fossils are arranged in their natural or zoölogical classification, preceded by the fossil plants where these occur in the same formation.

This arrangement affords a simple and satisfactory means of studying the fossils of each and every one of the Geological formations from the oldest fossiliferous rock to the base of the carboniferous system.

Upon the second floor the minerals of the State are systematically arranged in wall cases, and several cases are devoted to miscellaneous American and European minerals.

The floor of this story is mainly divided into three areas, in which are arranged representatives of the postpliocene vertebrata. Skeletons of the better known and more conspicuous forms of these arranged under the heads of " North American," " European and

Asiatic" and "South American." By this means the geographical relations of these extinct vertebrates are at once presented to the eye.

Upon the same floor are arranged a representative collection of the fossils of all the English formations, and of the American Cretaceous and Tertiary formations.

The wall cases on the south side of the room contain casts of remarkable fossil forms, mainly of European origin. These casts, with others in table cases, and those of the European and Asiatic, and South American areas were presented to the Museum by Charles Wadsworth, Esq.

The third floor of the building is devoted to the recent Zoölogical collections. The fauna of New York, in its birds and mammals, occupies the west end of the room; the DeRham collection is contained in a large central case towards the east end, while the New York fishes and reptiles occupy wall cases on the north and south sides of the eastern area.

The central area is occupied by table cases containing the Gould collection of shells, and the eastern area by table cases containing the Mazatlan collection of shells presented by Dr. P. P. Carpenter.

The collection of Antiquarian and Ethnological specimens occupies a part of the eastern end of the third floor.

Extensive additions and a partial re-arrangement of some portions of the collection will be made during the present summer and autumn.

The Free Museum and Stereoscopic Studio of Natural History, which was thrown open to the public, at 9 and 11 Elm street, in March of the present year, merits a highly complimentary mention here, and a visit from every one who sets foot in Albany. This enterprise was projected by Mr. Hurst, with the co-operation of his Son. For many years, Mr. Hurst has by his skill won golden opinions from the best judges, in Taxidermy. His own private collection—the result of thirty years' labor—is now open to the public, and fine Stereoscopic Views of the subjects are offered for sale.

The *New City Building* is a fine edifice, erected by the city in the fall and winter of 1868–9, at a cost of two hundred thousand dollars, on South Pearl street, corner of Howard.

It is a beautiful structure of the Lombardic style of architecture, ornamented with a Mansard roof, and is built of brick, faced with limestone from Lake Champlain.

Adjacent to this is Martin's Hall—a new building of which Albanians are justly proud. The Ball which honored its opening to the public was given by the Burgesses Corps of this city, on Washington's Birth-night, 1871, and was one of the blithest gatherings of "fair women and brave men" ever seen in Albany.

The *Trimble Opera House*, also on South Pearl street, is a building which has a "history all its own." It stands upon the site of the original "old theatre" of Albany, which was replaced by Trimble Opera House, so named after the late John M. Trimble, Esq., of New York, the famous Architect and Builder.

> Art, in our city, reared her Temple fair;
> But the Fire-Fiend—Evil Genii of air—
> Assaulted it with red, embracing wing.
> And smote it to the earth—a ruined thing !

People shrugged their shoulders and said that it would not be rebuilt—that it would never pay—plenty of gloomy prophesies were uttered over its ruins. For a long time, no effort was made to rebuild, till a man of enterprise, Mr. Lucien Barnes, of Albany, came forward, formed a stock company, and by tact, an indomitable will, and genuine hard work, erected and completed Trimble Opera House in *fifty-seven* working days, opening on the last day of the old year 1869. Truly was it written :

> Disjointed things his magic made cohere,
> That, called " Impossible," was swift begun ;
> In less than sixty days the task was done—
> Our Opera House assumed its peerless stand,
> Complete—" Star Theatre " of the land !

Retracing our steps to State street, at its junction with North Pearl, upon its northwest corner stands a venerable elm tree, which commands our attention. This tree was planted more than one hundred years ago by Philip Livingston, one of the signers of the Declaration of Independence. It was then merely a twig, and it is said that Mr. Livingston severely rebuked a young sailor, one morning, who was about to cut it down for a switch or a cane.

Upon the north side of State street, not far above North Pearl, stands St. Peter's Church. Here rest the remains of Lord George Howe, who was probably the most beloved of any British officer ever in command of American troops. He it was who said to a comrade : "Any gentleman officer will find his equal in every regiment of the Americans. I know them well. Beware how you under-estimate their abilities and feelings, civil, social and military." He was slain on his march to Ticonderoga, July 6, 1758. A monument was erected to his memory in Westminster Abbey by the province of Massachusetts Bay.

Forty-four years after his interment, a new place of worship was erected. The vault was then opened, and the decayed coffin of rich mahogany was revealed. It contained the ashes of the gallant dead, enshrouded in habiliments of gorgeous silk. The hair, dressed in the fashion of the age, was found to have grown several inches, and the ribbon that bound it was yet black and glossy. All, on exposure, seemed to shrink into dust.

ELM TREE CORNER, NORTH PEARL STREET IN 1805.

Fifty-seven years elapsed, and in 1859 the "Spirit of the Age" reared the beautiful gothic church which now occupies the ground. Again the sacred remains, inclosed by a double coffin, were revealed to view, and still the two pieces of ribbon which bound his hair together was preserved. Once more the coffin was inclosed by another, and placed in its receptacle beneath the church, there to remain, until at the bugle call, at the *Last* Reveille, his bones will start, and his soul will answer to the FINAL MUSTER.

Space does not admit of our tracing but a few of the links between the present and the past with which this old city abounds. The tourist who wanders among the one hundred and eighty streets of Albany, desiring to learn more of its associations, will find Munsell's Historical Collections of Albany, most valuable books of information and reference.

Tweddle Hall now stands near Livingston's elm tree, upon what was once known as the Webster corner, and from that noted spot cart-loads of Noah Webster's spelling books were scattered over Northern and Western New York. Upon State street, opposite the elm tree stood the Stevenson House, completed in 1780. It was then a wonder in architecture, being in a style quite different from anything in Albany. It was purely English throughout, its furniture was imported from England, and it was generally known by the distinctive title of "The Rich Man's House." There are many houses which might justly claim that title now in our old city.

Where Perry's Building, a fine new block upon North Pearl street, now stands, was once the Vanderheyden Palace. It was erected by one of the old burghers in 1725. The bricks and some of the other material were imported from Holland. It was one of the finest specimens of Dutch architecture in this country. The old mansion figures in Irving's "Bracebridge Hall," as the residence of Herr Anthony Vanderheyden. Its iron vane, in the form of a horse at full speed, now occupies the peak of the southern gable of Sunnyside. That gable is almost a complete fac-simile of the one of Vanderheyden's Palace, over which the vane turned for more than a century.

This fine old house was pulled down in 1833. The Baptist church which was reared upon its site has also bowed its head before the spirit of progress.

Let us hope that the old house upon Pemberton's Corner, at the intersection of North Pearl and Columbia streets, may long be spared! This building was erected in 1710, and for more than fifty years has been used as a grocery store. Whoever will step within, will be shown an oil painting of the house and its surroundings in 1710. Photographs representing its early days are also for sale there.

The name of Anneke Jans is as familiar to the ear as that of any American lady; but even Albanians, generally, are not aware that Anneke used to live at the corner of James and State streets, where Hurcomb now keeps his fashionable clothing store. She was buried in 1663, in the Middle Dutch Church yard, Beaver street. She had eight children, six of whom married and multiplied and replenished the earth at such a rate, that it is estimated, if their ancient farm in New York, now belonging to Trinity Church, and supposed to be worth several millions, was recovered and equally divided among all who claim to be her descendants, they would get about twenty shillings apiece.

Passing down Columbia street to Broadway, we notice that workmen are rebuilding the great printing house of Messrs. Weed & Parsons, which was destroyed by fire early in the present year.

VANDERHEYDEN PALACE.

More than three hundred workmen were thrown out of employment by this disaster. It was a fearful fire, destroying numerous stores and dwelling houses, but from its ashes have already arisen structures which forbid our regretting our losses.

We sometimes hear this age called the iron age; but recent advances in the application of paper to the arts would require a later and more significant cognomen. The "paper age" it is getting to be, in more senses than one. Paper collar manufacture has developed into a very large and important industry. Those who visit Albany, and have leisure to go over the Albany Paper Collar Company's establishment, at 621 Broadway, will be surprised and entertained by what they may see and hear. Of the seventy or more manufacturers in the United States, the Albany company, according to official returns, are excelled in capacity by only six. The cash capital of this company is over fifty thousand dollars, and working capacity of the factory is eighty thousand collars per day of ten hours. They give employment at their collar factory to from forty to fifty persons, mostly girls, and to about the same in addition, at the box factory of George N. Cozine, 283 and 285, Broadway, which is fitted up with all the latest improved machinery, and devoted expressly to making the little box into which the collars are put, each box containing ten collars systematically rolled in the least possible room. Ten of these little boxes are encased in another very neat box or cartoon, and in shipping, fifty cartoons are packed in regular sized cases adapted to the various styles of collars. These cases are transported to the remotest markets of the country. Their customers are to be found among the leading business houses throughout the north from Portland, Me., and Boston, in the east, to Omaha, Nebraska City and Leavenworth in the west; in the leading markets of the Southern States, in Galveston, at San Francisco on the Pacific, at Montreal,

Ottawa, Prescott, Kingston and Toronto in the Province Ontario, Canada.

It may interest some to know that four thousand boxes are daily filled by the Albany Paper Collar Company, the covers of which are ornamented with a fine representation of our new State Capitol. "Colfax" and "Red Cloud" are largely represented upon the boxes designed for western marts.

But to mention the manufactures of Albany would be an endless task. In every branch of industry, machinery is throbbing, and men are toiling to keep pace with the demands of the age.

The Albany Iron Works of Mr. Henry C. Haskell bear a fine reputation. The iron fence around the cathedral—over five hundred feet in length, and considered a splendid specimen of design and workmanship—also the iron bridges over the Erie canal nearly all through the State, have been manufactured here.

It is apprehended that Albany Beef, sometimes erroneously denoted Sturgeon, will at a future day be driven out of the market by the shad which Mr. Seth Green is artificially propagating, at the rate of a million a day, turning them into the river. And although shad are "Nature's pincushions for bones"—the interior of a shad looks like a fine tooth comb or a wool card, and the best way to get out the meat is to use a toothpick—Mr. Green's work will nevertheless be of great public value, affording to thousands a nutritious and wholesome article of food. The hatching grounds are on the Hudson, about ten miles from Albany.

The manufacturers of the "Cold Water Soap," another branch of industry, are busily engaged in supplying a brisk demand for this new article in twenty-seven counties of this State.

Some *live* State agents of Insurance Companies make this city their headquarters. Albany ale and Albany lumber are known everywhere.

Latham, "The" Hatter, opposite the Delavan House, drives as brisk and fashionable a trade as was ever known in the famous " English Hat Store," of olden times.

The Tontine Coffee House, that celebrated home for strangers and for gossips, which stood upon the site now occupied by Koonz's State Street Carpet Store, has been exceeded in prestige by the comfortable *Delavan*, of to-day.

And in place of the contracted printing office of the Webster Brothers, we have, besides those of lesser note, the great printing establishment of Messrs. Van Benthuysen & Sons, which was founded in 1812. This firm manufacture paper at their own mills, at Cohoes and Castleton. Their type is cast, their printing, press work and binding, is all done beneath one roof, which towers up well toward the sky.

What more shall we say of Albany? We have drawn but a rude and incomplete sketch where we desire to present nothing less attractive than an artistic steel line engraving. Many people will visit or make their home in Albany and note *only* its manufacturing interests, its churches and schools, the fine houses upon its hills, its places of modern resort and interest. They are interested only in the new houses, which tell of pride, prosperity or comfort. The old house whispers nothing to them of by-gone days. The ruin never calls in their hearing, "Come here and listen to my stories, there are secrets here yet." Men are alike, as far as *they* can see. The distinctions of dress, bearing, and personal beauty, are the only differences they note. Every individual of the species (unless he has lived in Mississippi) has two eyes; and unless he has been in the wars, or on a railroad, possesses two arms and two legs.

Beyond these appendages—into the peculiarities of race, education, and mental powers, which make one to differ from another—they never inquire. But let the student of human nature come to this venerable city, and *he* will discover here a strange medley of conservatism and enterprise, novelties and diversities of thought and deed, genial, independent, and sometimes obstinate and eccentric habits, looks, actions, and traits of character. Yet, urbanity and honor characterize Albanians. The stranger who is familiar with the ways and moods of people generally, in our large cities, will be charmed with the courtesy and kindliness shown him here. It is a city to be sought with pleasure, for a visit or a home, and only to be left with regret.

In closing this sketch of our Capital City, we are tempted to present a picture from the olden times. Many might be given which would amuse and interest our readers, but let *one* suffice. We extract it from " Random Recollections of Albany," published by Mr. Munsell, in 1866—a small volume which merits a more extensive circulation than it has attained.

In the early part of this century, Mr. Goldsborough Banyar, was widely known as one of the most intelligent, wealthy, and respected citizens of Albany. He was the most perfect type of the *Anglo-American* then living. The last of a race, or class of men, now totally extinct—a race born in England, grown rich in America, proud of their birth and prouder of their fortune. He had been a secretary of state under the colonial Government, and had performed the duties of his office in a manner highly honorable to his talents and integrity, and very advantageous to the province. Through his very long life he was considered a man of strict and unimpeachable integrity. At the breaking out of the war of the Revolution, Mr. Banyar, very naturally, and the prospect considered, very wisely, took sides (but not arms) with the mother country. He was a royalist in feeling, and doubtless in principle—the *feeling*, it is believed, underwent no change: the *principle*, in the course of time, became temperately, and we may add judiciously, modified by his own interests. He had, while in his office as secretary, obtained from the crown many valuable grants of land. These lands were the sources of his wealth. With the eye of intelligence, he watched the course of events, and like a skilful pilot, steered between the two extremes. He wisely kept a friend in either port, and had always an anchor out to windward. In short he preserved his character from reproach on the other side of the the water, and *his lands from confiscation* on this.

His mind kept pace with the intelligence of the age. He became an American when America became triumphant—thought better of Republicanism as it approximated to power; and finally, without abating one jot of his love for the land of his birth, came quietly into our political arena under the banner of Jefferson.

He was no American at the commencement of the war, but an Englishman born and bred, with the badges of office and confidence still in his possession.

Yet he took no part—gave no aid, and but little comfort to the enemy, for when secretly applied to, *for advice*, he sent by the messenger a basket of fruit—and when solicited *for information*, the return was a basket of eggs. He was therefore no *Tory*, but merely a judicious politician; in which character if he acquired no fame, he at least preserved his reputation and his property, and merited the thanks of those remembered in his will.

At the commencement of this century he must have been about three score and ten years of age. He was a short, stout built man, English alike in form, in character and aspect, and at this period was infirm, gouty and nearly blind, but still sound in mind and venerable in appearance. The colored servant by whom he was led, was no unimportant personage. He was his man Friday, his man Peter, his all-in-all, for without his aid locomotion was impossible. Peter resembled his master in every particular, save his gout and his blindness. He was of the same height and make, as well dressed, nearly as old, and quite as grey. He was, moreover, as independent, as important, and as irritable. Nothing could be more amusing than their conversations and disputes when moving together, arm in arm, down Pearl street, and across State to Lewis' tavern, upon the present site of 78 State street, a haunt to which they resorted daily when the weather would permit. Their dialogue was generally in a pretty sharp tone of voice, and almost always upon a disputacious key. In crossing State street, one day, on their return from Lewis', it commenced thus:—

" Peter," said the old man, " you're leading me into the mud."

" There's no mud here," says Peter.

" But I say there is," retorted the old man, fiercely.

" I say there ain't," said Peter.

" D—n it, sir," said the old man, giving his arm a twitch and coming to a full halt, " don't you suppose I know the nature of the ground on which I stand ?"

" No," says Peter, " don't 'spose you know any such thing; you ony stept one foot off the stones, that's all."

" Well, well, come along then ; what do you keep me standing in the street for ?"

" *I* don't keep you," said Peter," " you keep yourself."

" Well, well," come along," said the old man, "and let me know when I come to the gutter."

TRINITY CHURCH.

" You are in the gutter now," said Peter.

" The devil I am," said the old man; then pausing a moment, he added in a sort of moralizing tone, " there's a worse gutter than this to cross, I can tell you, Peter."

" If there be," said Peter, " I should like to know where 'tis: I have seen," continued Peter, " every gutter in town, from the ferry stairs to the Patroon's, and there ain't a worse one among them all."

" But the gutter I mean," said the old gentleman in a lower tone, " is one which you *cross in a boat*, Peter."

" 'Tis strange," said Peter, " that I should never have found it out : now lift your foot higher or you'll hit the curb-stone,—cross a gutter in a boat ! " ejaculated Peter, " 'tis nonsense."

" 'Tis so written down," said the old man.

" *Written down*," retorted Peter, " the newspapers may write what they please, but I dont believe a word on't."

" I'm thinking," said his master, " they put too much brandy in their toddy there at Lewis'."

" I thought so too," said Peter, " when you were getting off the steps at the door ; and since you've mentioned that boat I'm sure of it."

" What is that you say ? " demanded the old man, coming to a halt again, and squaring himself round ; you thought so, did you ? what right had you to think anything about it ? I tell you, Peter, you're a fool ! "

The attitude and appearance of the parties at this moment, was so whimsical—in fact so ridiculous, that a school boy who overheard this colloquy could not refrain from laughing aloud.

"Who is that?" said the old man, taking quietly hold of Peter's arm again.

"Don't know him," said Peter, "spose he's one of the *new comers!*"

"New comers!" said the old man, repeating the phrase. "Is he old or young, Peter?"

"Young," said Peter.

"Then I forgive him," said the old man: and after a short pause, added in a lower tone of voice, "*may he* never know the misfortune *of blindness or the gout.*"

However it was not at his infirmities that the narrator of this story laughed, but at the singular oddity of the scene, the ridiculous dialogue, and still more ridiculous attitudes of the party.

But enough of the reminiscences of the past. If these few pages tend to portray to the citizens of more distant parts of our State, Albany in some degree *as it was*, and *as it is*, our aim will be accomplished. Let us not keep the dates and meagre details of history, which are but the skeleton frame of life in other days, and let the recollection of the manners, customs and people that are gone, perish entirely from memory.

Opposite Albany lies GREENBUSH, formerly known as Het Green Bosch. East Albany, French's Village, and Bath-on-the Hudson, also lie on this side of the river, although all these villages are frequently (mis)called Greenbush.

Some of the residences in East Albany command views which are fully equal to any which can be obtained from the hills of Albany. One "Place" which we wot of there, has an outlook of the Hudson, and the open country upon the north. A full view of the stately city of Albany on the west, on the east the green woods, and on the south both the Helderberg and the Catskill Mountains. The grounds of this old place were once adorned (though not now), with *sixty-five varieties* of roses! Greenbush was formerly a portion of the Van Rensselaer Manor. Some old houses, and an ancient place of sepulchre, may be seen upon the river's bank.

In East Albany there is a Sulpher Spring of some note. Whoever will quaff a draught as it comes from the iron pump in the waiting room of the depot, will enjoy mineral water which tastes much worse than any of the waters at Saratoga. It is amusing to see the faces of unsuspecting travelers who alight, thirsty, from the passing trains, and having never tasted anything like this water before, devoutly hope that they never may again.

In 1866 a fine railway bridge was completed between East Albany and the city. Its cost was $1,150,500. In addition to this a magnificent iron bridge, light, airy and substantial, intended for the accommodation of passenger trains and foot travel, is rapidly approaching its completion in a more central location. By this bridge, trains will cross the river directly to the new Union Depot, which is to be erected in the rear of the Delavan House. These are improvements and facilities which the traveling public cannot fail to appreciate.

Aside from the Public Buildings which we have previously named in Albany, there are many others worthy of notice.

The *Dudley Observatory* was founded by the munificence of Mrs. Blandina Dudley, who expended upward of $75,000 in its erection and endowment. Other patrons of science have also liberally contributed to secure its prosperity.

It stands on Observatory Hill, near the northern limits of the city. It is built in the form of a cross, and contains some of the largest and finest instruments ever constructed. Among the instruments is a calculating engine made by C. Scheutz, a Swede, and purchased by John F. Rathbone. It is the only one in existence. A large class of calculations is performed by its use, and the results are impressed upon leaden plate ready to electrotype and print. Admission can be gained by application to the Trustees.

The *Albany Medical College*, which is a prosperous establishment with a fine museum, and the *Law School of the University of Albany* are on Eagle Street. They have the facilities for teaching the respective sciences.

The *Albany Almshouse, Insane Asylum,* and a *Fever Hospital* are located upon a farm of one hundred and sixteen acres, one and a half miles southwest of the city, and are under the management of the city authorities. The *Industrial School* building is located on the same farm.

The *Albany City Hospital*, on Eagle Street, was incorporated in 1849.

The *Albany Orphan Asylum*, on Washington Street, at the junction of the Western Turnpike, was incorporated in 1831; it was erected, was as the City Hospital, by private subscription; it is now aided by State funds.

The *St. Vincent Orphan Asylum*, incorporated in 1849, is under the charge of the Sisters of Mercy. The male department, two miles west of the Capitol, is under charge of the Christian Brothers.

There are upward of fifty church edifices. The Cathedral, upon Eagle street, with its four thousand sittings, and its fine, stained-glass windows—and the Church of St. Joseph, on Ten Broeck street—are perhaps the most prominent structures.

FIRST LUTHERAN CHURCH OF ALBANY, 1870

The State Normal School and Folsom's Business College are here—also a Male, and Female, Academy, and numerous other schools of more or less note.

At No. 5 Fayette Place, is the studio of the distinguished sculptor, E. C. Palmer, whose "Angel at the Sepulchre" has added so greatly to his earlier fame.

Above the city, on the flats, is the Schuyler House, a plain and antiquated dwelling. Here dwelt Colonel Peter Schuyler, the first Mayor of Albany, who took four Sachems of the Mohawk tribe to England, and created no small sensation by presenting them at the Court of Queen Anne. In 1759, it was destroyed by fire—the means of extinguishing fires at that day being chiefly, *that it rained sometimes.* The house was immediately rebuilt, however, and portions of the original walls are still standing.

In the northern part of the city, extending from Broadway to the river, surrounded by large and very beautiful grounds, is the Van Rensselaer Manor House, one of the most attractive town residences in the State. It is over two hundred years since the mansion of the first *Patroon* was built upon this spot, and some portions of the present house were reared in 1765. The horse cars which run between Albany and West Troy, pass this grand old place.

The Albany Rural Cemetery is accessible by these horse cars. It is situated on the Troy road, about midway between Albany and Troy. It stands fifth in the order of establishment of Rural Cemeteries in the United States. For beauty of natural scenery, it is not excelled, we believe, by any other in the country. In fact, there are Cities of the Dead which have been widely written of and admired, which are in every way inferior to this. The Albany Rural Cemetery is not a show-place. It is but little talked of. Its monuments are perhaps exceeded in expense, in many instances, by those of Greenwood, Mount Auburn and Laurel Hill—but in none of these places of note are the evidences of taste, care, and affectionate remembrance of those who have gone from us, more evident—in none are the flowers more profuse and beautiful—the rare and tropical plants more numerous or more carefully tended.

There is also very little of that monotony and sameness of style amid the marble and granite designs, which so often wearies the stranger in visiting a cemetery to which he has no especial or tender tie.

Among the finest monuments are the Banks Memorial, which shows a granite base, surmounted by "The Angel at the Sepulchre," that matchless work of our sculptor, Palmer. Probably the most unique and mournfully interesting stone is one of white marble erected to the memory of William H. Pohlman, Adjutant of the Fifty-Ninth Regiment of New York Volunteers, who died at Gettysburg, in the twenty-second year of his age. Stones of irregular yet harmonious shape are piled one upon another. Each stone bears the name of a battle in which the young hero participated—Gaines' Mills, Savage's Station, Bull Run, Yorktown, Fair Oaks, Malvern Hill, Fairfax Court House, Chantilly, Antietam, Fredricksburg, Turkey Bend, White Oak Swamp—the list is a long one, fearfully long for the young patriot of twenty-two.

Surmounting these *stone witnesses*, are his cap and knapsack, sword and the "dear old flag," all beautifully wrought in the marble.
"CEASE FIRING" is the sole inscription.

Not far distant is the monument bearing a medallion of the late Brevet Brigadier-General Lewis Benedict.

A very unique memorial marks the resting place of the lamented Dr. Alden March.

Beautiful designs abound and are far too numerous to be mentioned here. Upon the North Ridge there has been erected the Winslow tomb of such size as to be often mistaken for a small chapel. Its reputed cost was twenty-five thousand dollars. Near this tomb is a simple stone with this very significant inscription:

> "When this you see, remember me,
> And keep me in your mind;
> Let all the world say what it will,
> Speak of me as you find."

St. Agnes (Catholic) Cemetery is near the Albany Rural, and a glimpse of both may be obtained by travelers who pass over the Rensselaer and Saratoga road.

Albany and Susquehanna Road.

VI.

RAILWAY trains glide along like jointed reptiles, for the most part, through flat and uninteresting country. The passenger may *gobble half a view* here and there, just so as to provoke a slight desire to see "more." But the Railway Commissioner and Engineer regard the landscape as the last item to be considered in laying out a road. A short cut is of more consequence than a superb view. And so before the iron horse steams over its course—its career of mangling life and limb is inaugurated by a wholesale mangling of the beauties of Nature.

The Albany and Susquehanna Road is an exception to this general rule. It lies beside rocky cliffs which could not be entirely blasted away, and among scenery which an army of Engineers could not really spoil. It is also a road upon which very few accidents have occurred. Therefore the traveler may step upon one of its trains, with a pretty reasonable certainty of enjoying himself and coming out all right at last, at his place of destination.

Reader, we are bound to the Helderbergs. Until quite recently we know about as much of the Helderbergs—aside from the fact that we can see their peaks from our windows—as we know of New Zealand. From this state of ignorance we have emerged, and we propose now to impart the information we have gained, to those who are no wiser than we *were*.

And with a mental shiver we recognise the fact, that we cannot do justice to this unique Cliff region, without being very geological and quite scientific—but not absolutely stupid, we venture to hope.

In the State of New York are three principal mountain chains. The Adirondacks cover the northern granite region of the State, of rock which has been violently heated, if not melted, by the earth's internal fires. They are plutonic mountains, with peaks six thousand feet above the tide level. The Catskills are an isolated groupe of peaks on the Hudson, more than a hundred miles south of their granite elder brethren of the Adirondack. They are principally of the old red sandstones and shales which underlie the coal formation. These are sedimentary rocks, the silt of ancient ocean currents; their peaks exceed three thousand feet in height.

Between these, north of the Catskills, not twenty miles distant, is the line of small mountains known as the Helderbergs, the third though not the least of the mountain systems of New York. They are a long angular range of solid blue limestone cliffs, running nearly east and west. Their geographical name exists only in Albany County; but geologically, they are over three hundred miles in length, their unbroken strata reaching from the Hudson to Niagara and on into Canada. Their greatest altitude is one thousand two hundred feet.

These calcareous cliffs, filled with fossil, petrified sea shells, answer to the European Silurian and Devonian ages. By its peculiar fossil shells the Helderberg, like other rock, is known when met with in distant regions. In subterranean darkness it stretches, a hidden, undulating sheet of strata, an inner mantle to the continent, cropping out here and there, and leaving its wooded " Silurian ruins" to render picturesque the scenery of many a State.

In the far West a geologist picks up a fossil shell, examines it, and says, " Helderberg"—surmises that good limestone may thereabout be found, and gypsum for the plasterer's art, and iron pyrites —fool's gold—useful for sulphur and sulphuric acid manufacture. Caves also may be expected and sulphur springs are usually not far distant.

A Tennessee geologist also picks up a petrifaction and makes note of it as " Helderberg." And in Britain, Sir Roderick Murchison, mentioning the existence of his favorite Siluria in America, will not fail to dwell upon the Helderberg formation.

Yet it is very possible that of these three, not one has ever seen the Helderberg.

Recent excursions have been made thither by the members of the Albany Institute and of the Troy Scientific Association. A party of Editors have also recently found this trip in the highest degree enjoyable.

As we believe that excursions to the Helderbergs are to become fashionable, and also because we love to ramble away from the Beaten Path, we will in part transcribe our own experience, and in part avail ourselves of the scientific knowledge of one who has known the Helderbergs long and well, in portraying the wonders of this region.

" Helderberg " is a Dutch corruption of the old German *Helleberg*, meaning " Clear Mountain." This name was given by the first settlers of Schoharie County, who had the bold and distinct *bergs* constantly in view during their first day's journey westward into the wilderness. Though plainly visible, and but ten or fifteen miles from the ancient city of Albany, few of its citizens appear to know of their traditions and their beauties. Helderberg to many Albanians means "anti-rent," "sheriff's posse," military, blue uniforms, bright muskets and bayonets, and shackled prisoners, against whom no crime being proved they are always released.

Most of the farms on these hills were once called "manor land." It had its feudal lord and manor-house after the fashion in England prior to our Revolution. The farmers were peasantry, of whom feudal rents in the shape of wheat, chickens, and days' service were exacted, though the land was deeded to them, their heirs and assigns forever. Ignorant emigrants were led to invest their all, clear and improve the land, and give it value, not dreaming that they would have to pay the interest on their own improvements.

The Revolution came, the battles of liberty were fought, and down went Tory and Royalist. After that feudal exactions seemed hard and oppressive. Some now refused to pay the "quarter sale" —one quarter of the price received by the farmer each time a place was sold. If the farm was sold four times, the "Lord" received the cash value of the farm, and still pretended to own it! Threats not sufficing, they were called "Anti-renters," and war was levied upon them. The conflict is not wholly ended yet; but quarter sales are abolished.

The Susquehanna Railroad trains, as they leave Albany crowded with tourists bound for Sharon Springs, Cooperstown, or distant Pennsylvania, are forced to follow the wall-like precipices facing the Helderberg almost along their whole extent, far to the north and west, before they are able to climb it.

To those who desire to escape for a day from the oven-like city in summer; who wish to enjoy a scramble amoung romantic cliffs, in shady woods, beside cool waterfalls; to gather fossil corals and shells, to visit and explore the known caves, and search for new ones among the cliff ledges, the " Indian Ladder " region of the Helderbergs offer superior inducements.

Taking an early train on the Susquehanna Railroad and stopping at Guilderland Station brings one within a mile of the Indian Ladder Gap. Even from that distance the mountain spurs are visible. Wondrous are the deep, black shadows that they cast early in the day. A scarcely discernible zigzag ascending line, shows the Indian Ladder Road crawling up the mountain and along and beneath the precipices.

It is but an easy two hours' drive, however, from Albany, and many may prefer to visit it in the saddle or with a pleasant party. If the weather be dry and not very sultry the jaunt will well repay you. If your horses are brave and steady, you may drive up the mountain road—it is a mile to the summit—or you may lead your horses up, the party walking leisurely after. Still some descending team may be met, and it is ill passing on that narrow cliff road. Notwithstanding many accidents, this road is the highway, winter and summer, of the country folk.

If, however, you have a desire to " foot it," and wish to see the wildest scenery the place affords, abandon the road and follow the stream, called by some Black Creek, up the valley to the foot of the gorge—a savage stairway up the mountain slope, of broken rock-fragments and great water-worn boulders. Then, if your heart fail you not—for any place more difficult to climb is impossible— you will ascend for a breathless, dangerous, exciting three or four hours to the foot of the cliffs and the falls—an escalade which will bear comparison with anything climbable.

But you should not return without mementoes of your visit. Carry then a satchel, unless you have capacious pockets; for curiosities will meet you on every side. Besides the fossil medals of creation—petrifactions and minerals—the collector will find a thousand objects of interest.

Your satchel may contain some luncheon; a geogical hammer and a chisel would not be inappropriate; your sketch-book by all means. Gun or fishing-tackle here are useless; hunting there is none, save foxes, "coons," some ruffled grouse (partridge), and at times wild pigeons. The fishing is also poor, except for pickerel, perch, sunfish, and the like, in lakes and brooks amidst the hills back from the summit.

What is this Indian Ladder so often mentioned? In 1710 this Helderberg region was a wilderness; nay, all westward of the Hudson River settlements was unknown. Albany was a frontier town, a trading post, with Indians for beaver pelts. From Albany over the sand plains—Schen-ec-ta-da (pine-barrens) of the Indians—led an Indian trail westward. Strait as the wild bee or the crow the wild Indian made his course from the white man's settlement to his own home in the beauteous Schoharie Valley. The stern cliffs of these hills opposed his progress; his hatchet fells a tree against them, the stumps of the branches which he trimmed away formed the rounds of the Indian Ladder.

That Indian trail, then, led up this valley, up yonder mountain slope, to a cave now known as the "Tory House." The cave gained that name during the Revolution. The trail ended in a corner of the cliffs where the precipice did not exceed twenty feet in height. Here stood the tree—the old Ladder. In 1820, this ancient ladder was yet in daily use. There are one or two yet living who have climbed it. Greater convenience became necessary, and the road was constructed during the next summer. It followed the old trail up the mountain. The ladder was torn away, and a passage through the cliffs blasted for the roadway. The rock-walled pass at the head of the road is where the Indian Ladder stood. The Indians had once a similar ladder near Niagara Falls. There were probably many such among the cliffs. It was possibly the resemblance of this wild, mountain scenery to that of father-land far away that induced its early settlement by the Swiss, and gave the name of Berne to the neighboring town.

You have followed the rapid brook up the valley through the shadowy woods, and have reached a little prairie opening surrounded almost on every side by the great mountain slopes. It seems a window whereby the crag-climber may observe the whole extent of his labors. This spot was known as the "Tory Hook" or Plat, in days gone by.

Towering above the uppermost tree-tops are the gray, battlement-like cliffs. Many a dark recess and inaccessible ledge can be seen which human foot has never trod. Two lofty waterfalls stream down, milk-white, from the cliff-top at the head of each dry, rock-filled gorge. Your way lies to the right, up the gorge to the smaller of the two falls.

Following the stream, you commence the ascent of the gorge. It is no light undertaking. The bed of the stream is your best road; keep to the right. Difficulties begin; you are frequently compelled to cross the rapid stream on stepping-stones. At length you reach what may be termed the foot of the gorge. The stream rushes down in a number of little cascades—above it is lost amid the huge rocks. Look upward; your labor lies before you.

Up, then! Up! Ah! is it fatiguing? Look below! It seems easier to climb up than down. Retreat appears impossible, if not recreant. Upward, then! no longer over fallen rocks merely, but over prostrate cliffs rather. Huge blocks as large as little cottages or backwoods log-cabins are heaped in wild confusion; up them and over them! More toilsome, nay, dangerous, becomes the ascent; but now the novelty and danger give new zest, and "Forward!" shouts one. Whereat you all, with vigorous competition hurrying, climb and scramble upward; sometimes on foot, oftener upon hands and knees, and frequently prone, with aid of fingers and toe of boot, making slow progress up the face of some fallen mountain.

To climb, some aid themselves with sticks snatched up from where they were cast by the last great freshet that foamed down the wild gorge. Do not take each wriggling thing among the rocks to be a snake. One thinking to capture a serpent sunning himself on the rocks, found a sleek, fat eel! An eel there on those dry rocks? Assuredly. For, hark! do you hear that steady rushing sound, as of a subterranean waterfall? Hours of toilsome climbing have passed. Look upward, the falls are before you at last.

From the brink of the dark cliff drops a spray-white stream, about eighty feet, unbroken. Lost for a moment to sight it issues from a rocky basin, and ripples down in two streams brightly over a series of little stone steps, seldom over an inch in thickness. Suddenly the smooth descent ceases; the rock drops perpendicularly fifteen or eighteen feet. Down the face of this wall or "fault" dash two little cascades, hurrying down to lose their waters among the huge rocks of the gorge. This is the Small Fall, sometimes called the "Dry Falls."

Below (and on the cliffs above) this fall is one of the best localities for Helderberg fossils or petrifactions. Among these fossil shells of ancient seas are many peculiar to the Helderbergs. The names and features of these shells once mastered, two of the most important of geological ages are known to you. On the Pacific slope, amidst the Sierras, throughout the North American continent, even in foreign lands, knowing these fossils you will be able to recognize the Silurian and Devonian rocks. The Helderbergs are principally Silurian; above this, on the summit of the hills and on their southern slopes, Devonian rocks are found.

There is a stratum of the cliff rock, sometimes fifty feet in thickness, entirely composed of one variety of fossil shell. It is this that gives such interest to Helderberg precipices, more than to basalt Palisades, or even dread Wall-Face of the Adirondacks. If you are fortunate you may find the out-crop of that stratum and bring away a " chunk " of shells. A dozen or more varieties of fossils may here be found.

Eastward the path leads to the " Big," " Mine Lot," or " Indian Ladder Falls." Have a care when following this path; the overhanging rocks are often loose and trembling. Sometimes your mere approaching tramp will be sufficient to cause their rattling fall. Suddenly you turn a corner of the cliff, and pause in admiration of the scene before you.

From the edge of the overhanging precipice, more than a hundred feet above your head, streams down a silvery rope of spray, with a whispering rush, sweeping before it damp, chilly eddies of fugitive air, that sway the watery cable to and fro.

You may reach the cliff top from here by going further east, where the precipices decrease in height. Search till you find the ascent to a narrow ledge that leads to a square embrasure-like break in the cliff; it seems as though a huge block twenty feet square had been quarried out. In one corner you will discover the crumbling fragments of a tree ladder; it cannot exceed twenty-five feet to the summit. Ascend, and you will have an idea of the Indian Ladder.

Westward now along the cliff tops, back toward to the falls again, and the Indian Ladder road. You reach the stream which forms the Big or Mine Lot Fall, and, stepping through the bushes which obscure your view, stand upon the verge of the precipice. To your left, from the lowest ledge below, the fall leaps the cliff brink, and pours in a steady stream.

Recline here and rest. Six inches beyond your feet is the mossy, weather-worn, blackened cliff edge. Out beyond is empty air; below, the dark afternoon shadows of the perpendicular mountains are already casting the valley in shade. The wild, rock-filled gorges seem but tiny gutters; the forests shrubbery; all below miniature.

It is grand, thus reclining on the cliff brink, to view the widespread landscape to the north of the mountains—the joint basin of the Hudson and the Mohawk—a deep valley more than sixty miles in width.

Leaving the fall, westward again along the cliff tops, brings you to the Small Fall and a road; following this you come out upon another road. Look to your right: that deep angular cut through the rock is the Pass, the head of the Indian Ladder road.

Descend the defile; you are below the cliffs again in gloomy shadow. Here stood the Indian Ladder. Observe the semi-Alpine character of the road; off this built-up, wharf-like way more than one team has dashed. The trees on the long, steep slope beneath have their history: " The horse struck that one; the man was found just here."

As you descend the road the cliffs increase in height, and the Dome, a mantle-piece-like projection, fairly overhangs and threatens it. Climb the débris beneath the Dome and you will find a path. Follow it. It leads to a cave, the resort of Tories and Indians during the Revolution.

"The Tory House" is a large circular or semicircular cavity in the cliff, just above the road, a good view of which it commands. It is a single room, perhaps twenty-five or thirty feet in diameter, open on one side; looking out over a block of fallen stone—an imperfect rampart—down the wooded slope to the road, and beyond, into the deep valley between the mountain spurs.

Here Jacob Salisbury, a notorious royalist spy, is said to have been captured.

In the roof of the Tory House is a dark, spire-like cavity, which has, apparently, no connection with any other chamber or cavern. You may, returning, descend the mountain by the road, having seen the more prominent places of interest of the Indian Ladder region.

We now turn to the numberless Helderberg caves. To discover caves appears to require a cave-hunting instinct, a learned eye. The under-world has its peculiarities. It differs from the upper-world.

The limestone rock of the Helderberg is the cave rock of the world. Other names it may have beyond the oceans; but the rock is of the same age, and contains fossils similar to those found here.

Within thirty miles of the Indian Ladder one may count twenty caverns large and small. Among them, in Schoharie County, Ball's or Gebhard's Cave—brightest of alabaster caverns; and Howe's Cave, which strives to rival Kentucky's Mammoth Cave.

The caves of the Helderberg are not glittering crystal grottos, they are dark, damp and muddy. Among the cliffs, however, are some caves comparatively dry.

Sutphen's Cave, near the Indian Ladder, is reached by descending a narrow crevice through the rock to a ledge a few inches wide. Along this you crawl, the cliff above and below you, a dangerous path. Reaching a chill recess beneath overhanging cliffs, you are at the cave entrance. The cave is said to be of some extent, and perhaps it is—under water.

Westward, among the cliffs, above the village of Knowersville, is Livingston's cave, a small, dry, and romantic cavern. Should you happen to be near, it is worth a visit. West and east there are many more caves which you may find by seeking. Near the Hudson, toward Coeyman's, there are several.

At Clarksville, twelve miles from Albany, and eight or ten miles southeast from the Indian Ladder, are more caves. Two of these are well known; the entrance of one is in the back-yard of one of village houses. The subterranean river is the house well; a pair of steps lead down into a crevice in the rock. They have no other water. For drinking it is unsurpassed, but it issues from lime rock. This same river bursts forth near by in the bed of the Oniskethau, and aids that stream to run a saw and paper mill. Chaff thrown upon the river in the cave is soon found floating on the mill-pond. The stream empties into the Hudson at Coeyman's. It was once remarked that an amphibious animal might make its way through the caverns from Hudson River to Niagara Falls without once coming forth to daylight!

The " Half-mile Cave"—the larger cave, or the longer end of the cave, if they are but one—is about a quarter of a mile from the hotel in Clarksville. This cave is often visited, and has a large, wooden, cellar-like door, and wet, slippery steps, which lead in winter down into warm, steaming darkness.

Mind your steps; I speak literally. Now go down the dark hole on your right; it is a steep descent. You are in darkness again, and your lights but feebly illuminate the place. There is a sickening damp warmth; it is not unlike a charnel-house, a catacomb. Here is flint, there saltpetre; pyrites through heat will yield sulphur; the alders and willows from beside mountain brooks give choice charcoal. Here is gunpowder in the raw, for adepts in its manufacture!

You may have a mile or more of clambering in and out from this cave, and that is as good, though not quite so bad, as twenty-five miles. There are long passages where you might drive a team of horses and a wagon; narrow, muddy passages in profusion; bats, overhead and fluttering past you, everywhere.

The bats hang from the ceilings separately, and from one another in curious festoons. Aroused by your approach, some take wing and occasionally strike against your lantern, shattering the glass. On all sides you hear them squeaking and chattering and grinding their teeth; it is horrid. How they live there is a mystery; no suitable food is visible, and the door of the cavern is kept closed. Some of the bats seem withered and half dead; others are more lively. The gray or frosty bat is sometimes found here.

Cave explorations are interesting to those who love to see things before unseen, new and surprising. Who knows, some one thus exploring may discover a great, subterranean, transcontinental river; and underground, round-the-world canal, cheapening freightage between New York and San Francisco.

Winter is the best time to visit caves; it is certainly the most healthy season, for it is dangerous to enter a cold, damp cave in hot weather.

In winter the Indian Ladder or Mine Lot Fall is one huge icicle from the cliff brink to its base.

Frequently upon the brow of the mountain you will see a ruined tower perched; surprised, you draw near. The door is low and narrow, and seems to be almost closed by the débris; it has a very ancient look, and resembles some old feudal watch-tower you may have seen in Europe. The slope below is white with rubbish, and covered with fallen stone—the tower itself blackened with fire. It is a Helderberg lime-kiln. The lime made here is the best known; many of the poorer farmers burn lime in the winter. It replaces the charcoal burning of other regions, and though quite as laborious and scorching, is more remunerative. These lime-burners will tell you curious stories of the "animals" they have seen in the rocks; some of them have singular collections of the fossils.

The lime-stone, when blasted, breaks into large, regular blocks, well suited for building purposes.

Often the roads on the summit of Helderberg are of solid, level rock; the mountain top is a plateau as smooth as a table. Cantering along on horseback, the constant ringing clatter of iron against stone is painful. In places the rock is jointed and in small blocks, and resembles a Belgian pavement; again it changes, and a singular sight meets your eyes.

The rock plateau is split by numerous parallel crevices, stretching on either side in perspective; if you view them with half-closed eyes the dark clefts resemble railroad tracks. In storms the water rushes down into the caves below. On the mountain (above the village of New Salem) these clefts extend perfectly parallel for miles. The foxes also find excellent hiding places in these clefts.

The cave-country is not yet exhausted. Passing Esperance we arrive at Schoharie. Three miles from Schoharie is Howe's Cave. This cave was named in honor of its discoverer in 1842, Mr. Lester Howe.

Cave hunting at the East, is with many persons as much of a passion, as is cave owning in Kentucky—a taste exemplified by the late Colonel Croghan, who once said to a friend, in reference to the celebrated Mammoth Cave : " I bought it for four thousand dollars, and it has been a good purchase. I have been buying caves now this twenty years. The first one I owned was in Illinois, and now I own fifteen. People found that I was fond of caves and *they brought them to me* and I have bought them. They are curious things. *I always was fond of caves!*"

Mr. Howe must also have been fond of caves. From the various cavernous indications he imagined that there was a large cave in this vicinity, and at leisure intervals for more than a year made search for it. His visions were more than realized by the beauty of the subterranean world which he discovered. Its arches and walls reach away for miles, and Howe's Cave is probably still half unexplored. When the entrance was discovered the passageway was almost completely closed for almost a mile with gravel, clay and rocks. By closing the side water-courses these obstructions were washed away which otherwise it would have required years of labor to remove.

Over the entrance stands the Cave House, a pleasant hotel, and here from June to October a stream of visitors are constantly coming to see the cave. We are of the opinion that Howe's Cave will attain still a more extended fame. It is certainly the best worth seeing of anything of a similar nature in this part of the country. It is the Queen of the cave region of the Helderbergs where caves are plentiful, and range from the size of a quill to a mammoth.

Dressing for the exploration is always a comical affair—many ladies assume a guise unnecessarily ugly when we consider that the cave is usually dry during the summer months.

The first apartment visited in Howe's cave is the Lecture Room; forty feet wide—next comes Washington Hall—then the Bridal Chamber, where more than one wedding has " come off," including the nuptials of two daughters of its Discoverer. More than forty names have been bestowed upon different points here, and many of the places are well named, as Stygian Lake, over which we sail to Plymouth Rock.

Stalactites abound here and many of the fine effects of torch light illuminating walls and arches, columns and stalagmites, which are described by those familiar with the Mammoth Cave, are to be seen here.

Howe's Cave is said to rival or excel the Kentucky Cavern, but as we are not *fond of caves* and have never visited the latter we leave those wiser than ourselves to decide the mooted question.

The junction of the Cherry Valley, Sharon, and Albany Railroad is at Cobleskill. The distance thence to Sharon Springs is fourteen, and to Cherry Valley, the terminus of the road, is twenty-three miles.

The mineral springs of Sharon gush out from the bed of a small brook and from a steep wooded slope on its margin. Its Sulphur, Magnesia, and Chalybeate springs have acquired a just celebrity. For more than half a century their healing virtues have been known, but only since 1835 has Sharon been a place of popular resort. Upon the slope from which the fountains gush a curious phenomenon is exhibited. Within the space of a few rods are five different springs—Chalybeate, White Sulphur, Blue Sulphur, Magnesia, and pure water issuing from apertures which are in some cases very near each other.

The village is finely located, as it has been said, *in a valley on a hill*. Its nine hotels are always full, and the varied and lovely scenery around Sharon as well as the fame of its springs have enhanced the popularity of this fashionable resort.

CHERRY VALLEY is a pretty little village and is also quite a place of resort. It is noted as being the scene of a most sanguinary massacre in 1778, when the Tories and the Indians scarce spared one " to tell the fearful tale."

From Cherry Valley it is but a pleasant ride by stage or private conveyance to either Richfield Springs or Cooperstown.

The village of Richfield Springs lies upon a narrow plain, near the head of Canaderaga or Schuyler's Lake.

It has long been noted for the aristocratic and fashionable character of its summer guests.

The waters here are justly celebrated for their healing virtues. Hither the Mohawks came for the cure of frost-bitten feet; and tradition says that a famous healing prophet once dwelt upon a beautiful island in the midst of Canaderaga Lake to whom invalids from all the Iroquois used to come and leave their maladies. At midnight he would glide softly away in his canoe, penetrate the dark forest to the fountains, and then return to his patients with vessels full of the magic waters. He became proud and powerful; and at last he called himself the twin-brother of the Great Spirit. The blasphemy kindled the anger of the Almighty, and it consumed the boaster. One morning, when a bridal party went thither to receive the prophet's blessing, the island had disappeared. The Great Spirit in his wrath had thrust it, with the proud prophet, so deep into the earth that the waters of the lake where it stood are unfathomable by human measurement.

Lake Canaderaga is considered as beautiful as its name. It is five miles in length, and a mile and a quarter at its greatest breadth. Only one island breaks its surface, and there picnic and fishing parties resort almost daily in fine weather. All around the lake, the hills—partly wooded and partly cultivated—rise to a high altitude, except on the north, where, less than a mile distant, is the village.

From Richfield Springs the tourist may proceed by rail to Binghamton and thence to Utica by the Utica, Chenango and Susquehanna road—or from Binghamton may return to Albany. We propose to ride over to Cooperstown.

But Cooperstown, with its associations with the name of one of the first of American writers, is worthy of a chapter to itself, and it shall have it.

COOPERSTOWN.

VII.

THIS beautiful village, once the home of FENIMORE COOPER, and the scene of several of his *Leatherstocking Tales*, will well reward the Tourist, the seeker of quiet, rural beauty, of varied and picturesque scenery, of boating, fishing, etc., and of healthful summer residence.

The following description is abridged chiefly from the writings of FENIMORE COOPER, as to the village and vicinity, as they were a quarter of a century ago; with notices of subsequent changes, and of Cooperstown as it now is, from *The New York Evening Post* (edited by William Cullen Bryant & Co.) and other competent sources:

COOPERSTOWN was first settled about 1786, by Judge William Cooper, father of the author, since which it has remained a charming, but until lately, secluded and old-fashioned town. Now a wondrous change salutes the visitor. Luxurious cars replace the tedious lumbering stages; one excellent large hotel—the COOPER HOUSE—and half a dozen cheaper hotels and boarding-houses now

COOPERSTOWN, N. Y.
From the East.

open; another great hotel of the first-class now building; streets lighted with gas; a Young Men's Association, with Library and Reading-Room; a fine Public School; a fleet of boats, for sailing, rowing or fishing, and two steamers on the lake, running regularly and in connection with pleasure trips to the neighboring summer resorts of Sharon, Richfield, &c., which are reached in several hours, through varied and charming scenery. New York, Albany and Utica papers are received here on the day of their dates, and the telegraph connects with every quarter.

Cooperstown—the Capital of Otsego County, seventy miles west of Albany—has about two thousand inhabitants, and is now greatly enlarging and improving its attractions for both visitors and residents. It has six Churches, three Banks, two Newspapers and several manufactories.

A Sulphur Spring of moderate strength, already used in the village, and several stronger ones in the vicinity, are to be developed and utilized soon.

Cooperstown described by Cooper, in 1838.*

" The village is beautifully placed at the southern end of the lake, being bounded on one side by its shores, and on another by its outlet, the Susquehanna. The banks of both these waters vary from twenty to forty feet in height. * * * The place is clean, the situation is dry, and altogether it is one of the healthiest residences in the State.

Lake Otsego ('Glimmerglass').

" Lake Otsego is a sheet of limpid water, extending, in a direction from N. N. East, to S. S. West, about nine miles, and varying in width from about three-quarters of a mile to a mile and a-half.

---

* The headings of subjects are added by the Editor.

It has many bays and points, and as the first are graceful and sweeping, and the last low and wooded, they contribute largely to its beauty. The water is cool and deep, and the fish are consequently firm and sweet. The two ends of the lake, without being shallow, deepen their water gradually, but there are places on its eastern side in particular, where a large ship might float with her yards in the forest. The fish of the Otsego have a deserved reputation, and, at particular seasons, are taken in great abundance.

Picturesque Scenery.

"The shores of the Otsego are generally high, though greatly varied. On the eastern side, extends a range of steep mountains, that varies in height from four to six hundred feet, and which is principally in forest, though here and there a farm relieves its acclivities. The road along this side of the lake is peculiarly pleasant, and traveled persons call it one of the most strikingly picturesque roads within their knowledge. The western shore of the lake is also high, though more cultivated. As the whole country possesses much wood, the farms, viewed across the water, on this side of the lake, resemble English park scenery, and are singularly beautiful, even as seen from the village.

The Susquehanna River.

"Immediately opposite to the village, on the eastern side of the valley (for the Susquehanna winds its way for near four hundred miles through a succession of charming valleys,) the range of mountain terminates, heaving itself up into an isolated hammock, however, before it melts away into the plain.

Mountain Views.

"This rise is called the Vision, and its summit is much frequented for its views, which are unrivaled in this part of the country. The

OTSEGO LAKE.
From near the Cooper House, Cooperstown, N. Y.

ascent is easy, by means of roads and paths, and when there, the spectator gets a bird's eye view of the village, which appears to lie directly beneath him, of the valley, and of the lake. The latter, in particular, is singularly lovely, displaying all the graceful curvatures of its western shores, while the landscape behind them, embracing Piers, and the hills beyond, is one of the richest and most pleasing rural pictures that can be offered to the eye.

LIKE SWITZERLAND AND THE RHINE.

" Nothing is wanting but ruined castles and recollections, to raise it to the level of the scenery of the Rhine, or, indeed, to that of the minor Swiss views.

" The mountains south of Cooperstown form a back-ground of great beauty, and it is seldom that a more graceful and waving outline of forest is met with anywhere. The Black hills, in particular, are exceedingly fine, and are supposed to be nearly a thousand feet above the level of the lake.

CLIMATE. MOUNTAIN AIR.

"As the valley of Cooperstown is about twelve hundred feet above tide, it will readily be conceived that the summers are cool and the air invigorating. The lake causes a circulation of air, it being seldom that there is not a breeze either up or down this beautiful sheet of water.

VILLA SITES.

" The banks of the lake abound with eligible situations for country houses. On its western side, there is scarcely a quarter of a mile without one, and we feel persuaded that nothing but a good road to the Mohawk is wanting to bring this spot into so much favor as shall line the shores of the Otsego with villas.

A Resort of Elegance and Ease.

"We predict that Cooperstown, during five months of the year, will become a place of favorite resort for those who wish a retreat from the dust and heat of the larger towns. * * *

"The beauty of its situation, the lake, the purity of the air, and the other advantages already pointed out, seem destined to make it more peculiarly a place of resort for those who live less for active life than for its elegance and ease.

"Cooperstown is evidently destined to occupy some such place among the towns of New York, as is now filled by the villages and towns on the shores of the lakes of Westmoreland, in England, and by the several *bourgs* on those of the different waters of Switzerland."

The above is from *The Chronicles of Cooperstown*, edited and mostly written by Fenimore Cooper, in 1838.

Now that Cooperstown is brought within about four hours of Albany, Utica or Binghamton; that steamers are plying several times daily around the lake, in connection with cars for all points; and that the beautiful shores are offered by their various owners for building sites, large or small; the prophesy of Mr. Cooper seems approaching fulfillment.

Lake Glimmerglass in The Deerslayer.

In his *Deerslayer*, he gives a more poetic picture of the lake, as " a broad sheet of water so placid and limpid that it resembled a bed of the pure mountain atmosphere compressed into a setting of hills and woods."

"Cooper owed a part of his inspiration," said Edward Everett, "to the magnificent nature which surrounded him; to the lakes, forests, Indian traditions," etc.

LEATHER STOCKING FALLS.
Near Cooperstown, N. Y.

N. P. WILLIS, the Poet, once wrote an elegant and characteristic description of the beauties of this lake and village, which is too long to insert here.

HISTORIC ASSOCIATIONS.

In 1783, WASHINGTON wrote a friend that he had "visited the eastern branch of the Susquehanna and viewed the Lake Otsego." Mr. COOPER, in *The Chronicles of Cooperstown*, quotes the first number of *The Otsego Herald*, April, 1795, that "Otsego was originally the name of the lake, from which the town and county were named ; and that the term, among the aborigines, signified a place of *rendezvous* and of friendly greeting." Others say it signified "*The Beautiful Water.*"

The second newspaper ever published west of Albany—*The Otsego Herald*—was commenced here by Elihu Phinney in 1795. Its files are still preserved by his descendants.

Otsego Lake, the present village site, and the Susquehanna River, were the scene of interesting events during the Revolutionary War, when Major-General Sullivan sent General Clinton (father of De Witt Clinton), with a brigade of twelve hundred men, against the Indians. The incidents are recorded in *The Chronicles of Cooperstown*, and are now commemorated by a new drive near the river bank, south of the village, called the "Sullivan road." Traces of the old Continental road, then cut from the Mohawk to Otsego Lake, are still visible.

Prince Talleyrand, the great French Minister of State, visited Judge Cooper in 1795, when an acrostic in French, on Miss Cooper, appeared in the *Otsego Herald*, attributed to the pen of the great *Diplomat.*

Here Samuel F. B. Morse, then a young painter, spent a part of his youthful days, and amid these picturesque scenes cultivated the tastes which made him, later, President of the National Academy of Design, before he had become still more distinguished as the Inventor of the Telegraph.

Subsequently, among the residents here, were Colonel William L. Stone, editor of the New York *Commercial Advertiser*, and author of the Lives of Brant, Red Jacket, &c.; Thurlow Weed, the well-known politician; Ambrose L. Jordan, of the New York Bar; Major-General John A. Dix; Hon. Joseph L. White—one of the most effective stump orators of thirty years ago—Hon. Levi C. Turner, afterwards Judge Advocate under Lincoln; Professor George R. Perkins, once principal of the State Normal School, Albany; Rev. William Bradford, editor of the *Eclectic Magazine*, the New York *Evangelist*, &c.; Professor J. Finley Smith, of Hamilton College, and Hon. N. F. Doubleday, who here trained his son, afterward General Doubleday of Fort Sumpter; General George W. Morell and General John C. Starkweather of the army, and commander A. P. Cooke of the navy, were also from Cooperstown. Hon. Samuel Nelson, senior Justice of the United States Supreme Court, has resided here since 1825. The late President Nott, of Union College, in his younger days Principal of the Cherry Valley Academy, contributed matter for the press of the Messrs. Phinney, in Cooperstown, from which were after issued the revised Naval History and several other works of Fenimore Cooper, Judge Judge Hammond's Political History of New York, Stone's Life of Brant, an improved Family Bible, of which over two hundred thousand were sold; and many School-books of extensive circulation.

THE HALL.

The home of FENIMORE COOPER, at Cooperstown.

Views and Prospects Near Cooperstown.

From the upper floors of the Cooper Hotel, or from five to thirty minutes walk, a dozen prospects and objects of interest may be seen; and the drives on either side of the lake, by the river or over the neighboring hills, or to the adjacent resorts of Richfield or Sharon Springs, are varied and picturesque.

Among the favorite prospects and objects of interest within an easy walk, are Hannah's Hill, West Hill, Prospect Rock, Council Rock, Cooper's former Homestead Grounds, and his Grave, Lakewood Cemetery and Fairy Spring. Within two miles of the village, west of the lake are several charming prospects and the Leatherstocking (or Bear-cliff) Falls.

On the east side and nearly opposite, is *The Chalet*, a picturesque farm, once the property and favorite resort of Mr. Cooper, on account of its wild and Swiss-like scenery and prospects. A little farther up the mountain, here, is Leatherstocking's Cave.

Lakewood Cemetery.

Between the Chalet and the Village is the beautiful little rural city of the dead—Lakewood Cemetery—where, over shaded walks and drives, grass-grown graves and tasteful monuments, majestic pines sing the requiem of the departed.

Here sleep the remains of several whose lives were given to preserve their country's liberty in the late war of the Rebellion.

> "The muffled drum's sad roll has beat
> The soldier's last tattoo,
> No more on life's parade shall meet
> The brave and gallant few;
> On Fame's eternal camping ground
> Their silent tents are spread,
> And glory guards with solemn round
> The bivouac of the dead."

The Cooper Monument is a white marble column, some thirty feet high, executed by Launitz. The sculptures near the base include emblems of literary, nautical and Indian life, and on its capital is a statuette of Leatherstocking.

> "My glance took in an obelisk.
> High towering near the solemn wood
> Where Natty Bumppo's stalwart form,
> In lifted grandeur stood.
> Careless his hand the rifle grasp'd,
> That weapon known throughout the world ;
> And, crouching at the hunter's feet,
> His faithful hound was curl'd." *

POINTS OF INTEREST ON OTSEGO LAKE.

On the "Lake Glimmerglass" of Cooper's Deerslayer, the favorite resort for three generations of residents and guests—is still "Wild-Rose Point," three miles from the village on the west side. Here on green lawns and beside cool springs and winding brooks, under the shade of venerable oaks, parties of citizens and visitors are almost constantly found engaged in every kind of rural enjoyment. A mile nearer the village is Brookwood Point, now a summer residence, in a majestic grove effectively developed by tasteful improvement. The large farm of Judge Nelson (Senior Justice of the U. S. Supreme Court), lies between this and the village, and, like the adjoining lands, abounds in charming views.

On the east side, commencing at the Susquehanna, the spacious lawns and groves of "Lakelands" and the Bowers Farm and woods extend northward on the lake for a mile, with an attractive landing for Lakewood Cemetery ; then the varied shores of mingled lawn, forest, cliff and ravine of *The Chalet*, with a landing for Leatherstocking's cave. Two miles from the village is Point Judith, with its extensive lake prospects, its natural grove and

---

* From T. C. Latto's Poem on Cooper, in *Harper's Monthly*, July, 1870.

THE TOMB OF FENIMORE COOPER.
At Cooperstown.

tangled wildwood, in their primitive luxuriance. A portion of the lake shore above this slopes in gentle lawns to the water, while in most places, bold banks, dark wooded recesses and precipitous rocks form a foreground, east of which are found terraces fringed with forest and grove, bounded by steep hills, and commanding those charming views of the lake, its varied western shores and farms, and of the village whose beauties Mr. Cooper has described in the extracts already given.

Our space will not allow us to go farther from the village in our details, but the steamers and smaller lake-craft are daily making the circuit of a score of scenes of picturesque beauty and of classic association around the lake.

OTSEGO LAKE STEAMERS AND OTHER CRAFT.

The new steamer "Natty Bumppo," just completed for the season of 1871, by A. H. Watkins & Co., will be a great luxury and convenience to summer travelers and guests. Accommodating three hundred passengers, embracing all modern conveniences and improvements, it will make several pleasure trips daily around the lake, and also connect regularly with trains of the Cooperstown, Albany and Binghamton Railroad on the south, and by stages with the Richfield Springs and Utica and Central Railroad on the north. Sharon Springs and Cherry Valley are but seven miles from Otsego lake.

Capt. Cooper has always a large fleet of sail and row-boats; Captain Boden—son of the old Commodore of the lake—has another fleet, and the "Mary Boden," a small steamer; all of which furnish abundant facilities for parties large or small, enjoying the lake and its shores at any moment. Messrs. Thayer & Tunnicliffe have acquired a reputation for their fish dinners, at the three and five mile points on the west side.

ACCESS TO COOPERSTOWN.

In connection with the above, it may be stated that Cooperstown is reached from Albany or Binghamton in about four hours, twice daily, by rail; and from Utica and New York Central railroad on the north, by railroad to Richfield Springs, thence by stage and steamer to Cooperstown in about four hours.

COOPERSTOWN IMPROVEMENT ASSOCIATION.

This society, which includes Judge Nelson of the U. S. Supreme Court, and all the most prominent citizens, is doing much to increase and develop the attractions of this village and vicinity. Its several Committees have in charge the increase and extension of varieties of the lake fish; the improvement and beautifying of points of prospect on the lake and hills, paths, drives, &c.; developing sulphur springs; planting of trees; prevention of nuisances, &c.

Besides several elegant residences now in progress, an Episcopal Orphan Asylum of tasteful design, in brick, is to be erected in 1872, on a commanding mound in the south west part of the town. A Hygienic Resort, to furnish an attractive home for invalids and seekers of health, is also in contemplation. The Otsego Co. Agricultural Society will soon improve their beantiful site on the Susquehanna, half a mile south of the village. Much building and improvement have been and are going on in this south west portion of the town.

FUTURE IMPROVEMENTS.

The Air-line railroad connecting New York and Ogdensburgh on the Canada line, now two-thirds built, passes through Cooperstown and will shorten the distance to New York nearly one hundred miles. The inhabitants of Fort Plain and vicinity on the New York Central railroad, also contemplate connexion with Cooperstown by rail.

The head-waters of the Susquehanna River, at Cooperstown, and numerous smaller streams, offer convenient water-power for manufactories here; while the division of several large farms adjoining the village into building plats of every variety, favors the erection of residences, business depots or factories. For the latter, sites are now in market on the railroad and river; and these lands are now in so many different hands, as to insure a healthful competition in prices.

On several eligible sites, tasteful cottages are to be erected and furnished, in 1872, for summer rent. As living in Cooperstown has not yet reached the high prices of other summer resorts, those who would consult economy in their pursuit of health and fine scenery, will be comparatively well suited here.

The New York Home Journal says of Cooperstown: " Lying in what may justly be termed the Paradise of Central New York, its locality is unsurpassed for the beauty of its scenery and the healthfulness of its climate. Otsego Lake, for picturesque surroundings and historical interest attaching thereto, equals Lake George."

TROY, BALLSTON, SARATOGA.

VIII.

TROY is a lively, bustling city, with plenty of enterprise and fashion within its limits. This Trojan city likes to boast, and it can justly do so, that it is ahead of Albany in certain respects, while Albany pursues the "even tenor of her way," without much concern as to what Troy may be about.

The two cities differ as widely in many aspects as they could do if they were separated by miles of land and sea. But comparisons are always odious, often invidious. Let us have none of them! The cherry should not be underrated because grapes are with some a favorite fruit—nor the elm tree of our own soil be disparaged by those who sit in the shade of the chestnuts of the Buckeye State. Troy has large manufacturing interests.

It has a population of nearly fifty thousand souls. It has residences in which style and luxury are most pleasingly blended with the charms of refined homes.

It is overlooked upon the east side by classic Mount Ida, and upon the north by the barren heights of Mount Olympus, two hundred feet high. There are country seats upon Mount Ida which command a view of *ten towns* in several different counties.

The Episcopal churches of St. Paul and St. John are fine specimens of church architecture. Since 1821, *Mrs. Willard's* School has added to the prestige of Troy. Here the Davidson sisters attended. Here was gathered the first class of young ladies ever instructed in the higher mathematics in this country. This was the pioneer young Ladies' Seminary of the land.

The Sorosis soon after the decease of Mrs. Willard appointed a committee to carry out a plan of an Emma Willard Fund, in memory of Madame Emma Willard, the educator and friend of her sex. The fund to be applied to providing a perpetual scholarship for some needy but meritorious young girl in an institution selected and approved by Sorosis. An admirable memorial truly—but as far as we can learn it has been only projected.

Oakwood and Mount Ida Cemeteries are worthy of a visit. In Oakwood upon the 8th of April, 1870, were deposited the mortal remains of General George H. Thomas. A ribbon of immortelles and wreaths of ivy had been twined around the edge of the casket in California, and went with it in the grave. His widow still resides in Troy. It was by her request that no panegyric or eulogy was pronounced over the coffined form of the indomitable soldier who once kept "pounding away" at Chickamauga.

WEST TROY is the seat of a large United States Arsenal. More than thirty buildings are located here, in grounds which comprise one hundred acres. West Troy is also noted for its Bell Foundries and other manufactures.

The Falls at COHOES are very beautiful. The Erie canal rises by a series of eighteen locks from the Hudson river, through the city of Cohoes, to the northerly part of the town of Watervliet, at which point it crosses the river in a magnificent stone aqueduct. The products of the manufacturing interests of Cohoes amount to more than two million dollars annually. In recent excavations made in the rocky banks of the Mohawk, the fossil remains were discovered of a gigantic Mastodon. A liberal public spirit prompted its presentation to the State collection at Albany.

* * * * * * *

The Rensselaer and Saratoga Railroad.—Under this name are associated six different Railway Companies, all under one control and management. These associated roads form portions of the great direct through routes from New York to Montreal, by the way of the valleys of the Hudson river and Lake Champlain. This route also forms the avenue to the popular watering places of Ballston, Saratoga and Lake George, and is the great thoroughfare of summer pleasure travel.

At Round Lake upon the Saratoga road, about forty acres of ground are held as the property of the Round Lake Camp-Meeting Association, of the Methodist Episcopal Church, Troy Conference —which was incorporated about two years ago by the State Legislature. Delegates from the conferences of twenty-eight States of the Union met here last summer, and at one church service the immediate audience numbered eight thousand persons. The sermon was delivered by the eminent Bishop Simpson, and well might one worthy brother exclaim—as he was heard to do—" if we could not *all* hear, we could *all shout Amen!*"

Ballston Spa has been long noted for its springs. A log-house for the accommodation of invalids was erected here in 1792 by Benajah Douglas, the grandfather of the late Hon. Stephen A.

TABLE ROCK FALLS
Above Troy, on the Hudson.

Douglas, but of late years Saratoga has greatly overshadowed Ballston.

SARATOGA.—We arrive here—with the multitude—at last. There are here really a half dozen different Saratogas, and each one attracts its own "set." Here, young men come with "fast" teams and a keen interest in pretty faces and—*the races*. Hither wend the fop and the flirt, whose paradise is the ball-room; this realm is ruled by the millionaire and the managing mother. Then too there is a Saratoga of the sportsman. Also a Saratoga of the invalid.

Outside of all these Saratogas, there is still another, which attracts thousands of sensible, healthy, but busy and overworked people, who come here every year for genuine recreation.

"The time to come," says a correspondent of the *Evening Post*, "is early in June. With an average of say six waiters to each guest, there is a certainty of getting something to eat, and the dinners daily offered at the best hotels are by no means to be despised; horse hire is at least one-third cheaper than it will be ten days from now; the small but beautiful parks are not yet thronged, and there is plenty of elbow-room on the broad piazzas of the hotels. One need not wait now for water at the springs; the willing and nearly idle boy has filled the tumblers before the drinkers have fairly entered the enclosure. A party of four or five can almost monopolize any one of the three hotels at the lake for the whole afternoon. In short, Saratoga, its springs, its hotels, its waiters, its livery establishments, everything that can contribute to the comfort and convenience of the pleasure seekers, is for a time, wholly the property of the few who are already here. This is the picture upon the third of June! How will it be on July third?"

But to most people Saratoga without its crowds would be divested of more than half its charms. Saratoga is a social exchange. It is a place for pleasure—a perpetual festival.

It is estimated—so says an exchange—that the visitors at Saratoga expend about an average of twenty million of dollars annually! The local population is about nine thousand, while in summer one thousand visitors a day oftentimes "enter into possession."

In all the hotels and private boarding houses collectively there are not far from seven thousand eight hundred rooms. The amount of provisions consumed by the occupants of these rooms is something marvelous, and we cannot spare room for details; but it may be interesting to know that at one single hotel, last season, two millions of tooth-picks were—used up!

More than thirty mineral springs attract summer guests, and establish the reputation of Saratoga as one of the most famous watering places of the world.

It has been suggested that the Pool of Bethesda was the first mineral spring whose virtues are recorded.

It is certain that the Greeks used mineral waters for drinking as well as for bathing; and the luxurious Romans were accustomed to spend their summer months at the once famous watering place of Baiæ, where a mild climate, a sheltered coast, and delightful scenery combined their attractions with those of the waters whose healing powers had then a world-wide celebrity. In the old world, the springs of Harrowgate, Cheltenham,. and Bath in England, Seidlitz in Bohemia, Spa in Belgium, Baden-Baden and Seltzer in Germany, and Aix-la-Chapelle in Rhenish Prussia, while they are of very ancient renown, are at this day annually resorted to by thousands of fashionable and wealthy pleasure seekers, as well as by invalids of almost every description.

The High Rock is the oldest and most famous spring in Saratoga. It was the Bethesda of the Indians, and by them used and regarded with superstitious reverence, long before a white man tasted its waters. It is believed to have been the first spring to attract the attention of the Indian hunters—it was also the first of which they spoke in praise to the white pioneers.

The water has built a curb for itself, the foundations of which must have been laid when the Continent was in its infancy. The water being impregnated with particles of mineral substances, probably at first saturated the ground about the outlet of the spring. As it evaporated, a species of rock was formed by the commingling of earth and mineral; successive though almost imperceptible deposits overlaid this formation, and in the course of ages the foundation of pure mineral substances was laid; and the water continuing to flow over its surface, gradually built up the present phenomena of nature.

It is said that the first white man who used these waters was Sir William Johnson, who was brought through the wilderness which then surrounded Saratoga on a litter, and remained drinking the water for a few weeks, when he was able to walk away without assistance. This is the first recorded instance of the thousands of well authenticated cures effected by the waters of Saratoga.

There is an Indian tradition that many years ago the water ceased to flow over the rock, owing to the displeasure of the Great Spirit. The water, however, remained within reach from the top, and the overflow probably found a way of escape through cracks which eventually have been stopped by deposits from the water. Man, however, took it upon himself to assist nature, and in 1866 an excavation was made below the rock. Immediately under the rock was a tree-trunk eighteen inches in diameter, still preserving its shape, but not very firm in its texture. Directly below the outlet was a cavity some ten feet deep, in which were found a large number of tumblers, cups, etc., which had, in the course of years, slipped from careless hands and been lost. The water was traced to the point at which it issued from the solid rock, tubes were set to bring it pure from its source, and now the High Rock is a favorite resort for visitors. The bottling-houses near by contain the usual apparatus for preparing the water for foreign markets.

By connoisseurs in the mineral waters of Saratoga, it is often and, we believe, truthfully stated, that the High Rock Spring water is less injured or affected by bottling than the generality of the waters at Saratoga. Analysis sustains this recommendation, by proving it to contain a large proportion of *fixed* carbonic acid gas. The recent tubing, which is about ten feet south of the old spring, has greatly improved its quality. It is bottled and sent everywhere. Upon the Pacific railroad, as well as upon our Eastern roads, boys go through the trains shouting: " 'Ere's your celebrated High Rock Water!" It is sold equally in San Francisco and in cities nearer home.

Deposits of mineral matter similar to the calcareous tufa, which constitutes High Rock, have been found at the surfaces of other springs, but this—

IS THE GREAT SPECIMEN.

The following are the dimensions of the rock: Circumference, twenty-four feet four inches; height, three feet six inches; diameter of aperture, four inches—below the top, one foot; weight, about eight tons.

The rock is a hollow cone or pyramid, whose walls are of nearly even thickness. More than one footstep is pointed out upon its side—a curious circumstance which tends to prove the theory which has been advanced by scientific men as to its formation.

Of the genuineness of this rock there can be no doubt. Thousands of years were necessary for its formation, which can be traced by the rings or circles of deposit marking each year.

The proprietors of the High Rock Spring have issued a very interesting pamphlet, containing a full account of the High Rock, and a history of the spring.

There are other wonders for us to examine, and we must pass on, commending the little work to which we refer, to our readers. It may be obtained, free of charge, at the spring, or will be sent by mail to those who address the High Rock Spring Company.

In 1868, a fine pavilion was erected over the spring at a cost of five thousand dollars.

South of the High Rock, is the Seltzer Spring. Our worthy German citizens rejoice in this spring, the water of which is almost identical with that of the famous Nassau Spring, in Germany.

The Saratoga Star Spring is a few rods north of the High Rock. The recent inventions of Mr. Putnam, the Superintendent of the Company, for bottling the water, are attracting much attention. These improvements are not yet fully developed, and will, it is anticipated, in a little time completely revolutionize the time-honored processes of bottling which are now in vogue.

The Empire Spring is a few rods above the Star Spring, but contains a less quantity of mineral constituents.

The Red Spring is near the Empire. It is more than a century old, and of acknowledged medicinal value, which has not been properly appreciated till recently.

The Excelsior Spring is about one mile northeast of the village and the springs just mentioned. It is a

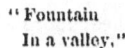

"Fountain
In a valley."

with pleasant scenery and fine woods for a surrounding.

The water of the Excelsior Spring is thought to be fully equal to any water in Saratoga.

It flows directly from the primeval rock (through a tubing fifty-six feet in depth), and is thus obtained of great purity and excellence, and with a very large amount of carbonic acid gas, rendering it a most agreeable water to the taste, and increasing its efficiency.

The medicinal agents which it contains are held in such perfect solution, that the water will remain clear and free from sediment or deposit in any climate.

For shipping, the Excelsior Spring water is conveyed into reservoirs, by its own hydrostatic pressure, thus retaining the full amount of carbonic acid gas which exists in the water naturally.

The Excelsior water is then shipped from Saratoga in these gas-tight reservoirs, lined with pure block-tin, and is forced out from them precisely as it flows from the spring, without charging it with gas.

In the immediate vicinity of the Excelsior are the Ten Springs, of which we shall doubtless hear more some day. They are undeveloped as yet. Hathorn Spring is on Spring street, just above Congress Hall. H. H. Hathorn is the proprietor.

This spring has the most central location of any in Saratoga. It was discovered and tubed in 1868. It is very similar to the old and well known Congress water, but is now considered superior to it.

Congress Spring is in Congress Park, on Congress street. It is famous as one of the oldest springs of Saratoga.

Columbian Spring is also in Congress Park. It is a strong tonic, and if taken too freely is apt to win for the Columbian, the title of "The Headache Spring."

The Pavilion Spring commands a wide popularity. It is in a central location, only a few steps from the business portion of the village and from the principal hotels. Although discovered at an earlier day, it was not tubed till 1839. Its waters are having an extended sale.

The United States Spring is a comparatively new spring near the Pavilion. The Hamilton is near the Hathorn. Washington Spring is in the grounds of the Clarendon Hotel on South Broadway. It is sometimes called the Champagne Spring, on account of its sparkling properties. This is one of the most pleasant waters of Saratoga and is a superior tonic. The grounds in this vicinity are fine, and during the season are thronged with the beauty and fashion of Saratoga.

In the same grounds and within a few rods, is the Leland Spring, named in honor of the genial proprietor of the Clarendon.

The Crystal Spring is in Park Place, Broadway. C. R. Brown, proprietor. This spring was discovered and tubed in 1870, since which time it has become widely known.

Eureka Spring and the famous White Sulphur, are situated on Spring avenue a mile and a-half distant. The latter is considered the finest sulphur spring in the State.

The Geyser or Spouting Spring must complete our list, which is surely long enough, of the principal and popular waters of this summer resort.

The Geyser or Spouting Spring was discovered in February 1870. There had been indications of mineral springs in this neighborhood for a long time ere its present proprietors decided to bore for a spring. Reaching a point one hundred and forty feet below the surface rock they struck the mineral vein. The water instantly burst forth, establishing the phenomena of a Spouting Spring.

As the water is drawn from the spring, it foams like soda water, and is of a temperature only fourteen degrees removed from the freezing point.

The Geyser is located nearly two miles from the village upon the Ballston road.

At Saratoga it is the rule to drink a quantity of the waters before breakfast in the morning. Some people, however, seem to have no idea of the propriety of limiting themselves at all, but exhibit a camel-like capability of drinking as much in one day as should be a whole week's supply. Six glasses half-a-dozen times a day is rather too much even of a good thing.

The leading hotels of Saratoga are well known. The superb Congress—the magnificent Grand Union—which will accommodate more guests than any other in the world, except one—the *enjoyable* and more select Clarendon, with its Washington spring, and its grounds lighted with gas.

The fame of Saratoga as a watering place is probably fully equalled by its reputation as a health resort. In the latter point of view its advantages are not merely its wonderful "Great Medicine Waters," but its climate is peculiarly salubrious. Upon the north and west the Kayadcrosseras mountain affords protection and shelter, and the Green mountain range on the east, with the Catskills on the south, form a mountain bulwark around the place to shield it from the cold and strong "wind and tempest."

Thither come the pilgrims who seek not the Fountain of Youth, but the Fountain of Health. For many years "Doctor Bedortha's Water Cure" was widely known as the only Remedial Institute in the place. Many New York families sent their invalid members here. Noted people from all parts of the country made the "water cure" their Saratoga home. There are now other establishments of a similar nature, but Doctor Bedortha is still at his post. His establishment is in connection with the Park Place hotel, where a magnificent building is projected and partly built. It is expected that visitors in 1872 will see these plans fully carried out. Meanwhile *Doctor Bedortha's Water Cure* is patronized by large numbers from all parts of the country, and has a wide-spread name. The rooms to be found here are as airy and eligible as any in Saratoga, and the Crystal Spring is upon the grounds of the establishment.

The Crescent Hotel, under the management of Doctor Hamilton, is a favorite resort in Saratoga. Although a medical institute is connected with it, it is entirely free from any objections that may be supposed to pertain to such, but is rendered more desirable thereby. Doctor Hamilton is also widely known as a skillful and successful physician.

Aside from the larger houses, Saratoga abounds in small hotels and private boarding places—it must be remembered, however, that a hotel of small accommodations at Saratoga would be considered *large*, almost anywhere else. There are buildings here which have received from seven to nine alterations and additions, and still the work goes on and the people cry—more, more, more room. In fact the *suburbs* of some of the older houses cover much more ground than the original structures. Cupid is a presiding officer at Saratoga. Many a "Diamond" wedding has been celebrated of which a Saratoga engagement was the avant-courier. Among other matrimonial incidents of note, it is said by gossip that the acquaintance of Commodore Vanderbilt with his present wife, commenced at Saratoga, and that very naturally the bridal party turned their faces Saratogaward immediately after the marriage ceremony.

The most fashionable drive is the new boulevard to the lake. This drive is four miles in length, with a row of trees on each side and one in the middle. Carriages pass down on one side and return on the other. For a long time it has been the principal drive in Saratoga, but until recently there have been few attractions besides the gay and brilliant stream of carriages with their fair occupants and superb horses. Since last season immense sums of money have been expended on the avenues and roads in the vicinity of Saratoga, and this new boulevard is a magnificent drive.

Moon's Lake House, upon a bluff fifty feet above the lake, is one of the resources of Saratoga. Its *specialty* is Fried Potatoes, and they are prime—are sold in papers, like confectionery.

Chapman's Hill, Wagman's Hill and Hagerty Hill, all afford fine views of the country. About a mile above Congress Hall, the half-mile track and the handsome grounds of Glen Mitchel are located.

Bemis Heights, the Saratoga battle-ground, are about fifteen miles distant, in Stillwater. Here occurred the famous engagement between Burgoyne and General Gates; and thousands annually stroll over, and moralize and flirt, upon the " Old Camp-Ground.

The most extended view and the boldest landscape may be seen from Waring Hill, upon the Mount Pleasant road, fifteen miles from Saratoga.

As the Press of the country has teemed with accounts of the splendors of Morrissey's Club House in Saratoga, we wish to correct some of the false impressions which are afloat concerning it. We copy and present below a *reliable* statement of this establishment, from the pen of Mr. R. F. Dearborn, the admirable Saratoga Correspondent of *Our Society* and other publications.

" Few are the journals of city or country," says Mr. Dearborn, that have not contained some notice or account of Morrissey's Club House. It has become one of the first objects to which the attention of visitors is attracted. A very exaggerated idea of its magnificence has been excited by so much talk and the glowing accounts of the *penny-a-liners*. For instance, we were told that one of the 'very finest' oil paintings in the country adorned its walls; but when we came to investigate, we learned that the expense of this 'magnificent work of art' amounted to about three thousand five hundred dollars. We concluded that either Mr. M. was exceedingly shrewd in purchasing, or else the finest paintings were at a discount.

"The building is very substantial, and is well furnished. That its furnishings are superior or equal to the first-class residences of our cities, is by no means true. During the past winter a large addition has been made to it, the main object of which, it is said, is for the selling of pools for the races. This is by far the finest part of the building.

"The case of the Young Men's Christian Association *vs.* Morrissey remains yet undecided, but that Association closed three other establishments for the same purpose. During the winter and spring, such efforts have been made by leading citizens to restrain, within proper bounds, the vices and crimes incident to any fashionable resort, that it may be hoped that Saratoga will become the most moral, as it is now the most celebrated watering-place in the world. Large numbers of the most highly cultivated, as well as the most wealthy people are among the summer residents of Saratoga, and a majority of its citizens will sustain this action for the suppression of open vice."

Guests who tarry late in the season at Saratoga, are well rewarded by autumnal sunsets, which are cold and gorgeous like the splendor of October woods. But as clouds dim the waving of golden grain, so a shade of melancholy touches those who go away when the last polka is polked—the last light in the last ball-room is extinguished, and the summer ended.

But we are not of those who tarry for September lights to crown the purple hills of the horizon. We have but lingered here a day, and before us lie the shores of Lake George and the grand expanse of the mighty Wilderness.

THE LAKES, THE ADIRONDACKS.

IX.

LAKE GEORGE may be reached by more than one route, but there is an inevitable stage ride of nine miles to be encountered or enjoyed—according to the temperament of the traveler. Of the trip to Lake George via the Adirondack railway, we shall speak hereafter. We shall follow now the usual track of those who visit Lake George only.

This is from Saratoga to Glen's Falls by railroad, changing cars at Fort Edward. Upon the old stage road from Fort Edward to Sandy Hill, until 1852, there stood a majestic pine-tree. In 1848, it was said by one who saw it, that an unaccountable decay had stripped it of its emerald robe, and left it standing, spectre-like, on the border of a woody glen. Its top had been broken off by a November gale, and its more delicate branches were falling at the touch of every breeze. Upon its huge trunk, full fifteen feet in circumference, was carved in bold letters—

"JANE M'CREA, 1777."

It stood on the brow of a slope covered with shrubbery and small trees, at the foot of which bubbled a clear and copious fountain called " The Jane M'Crea Spring." The hollow was called " The Jane M'Crea Glen." The name of the damsel seemed to be audible in the rustle of every leaf, in the chirp of every grasshopper, and in the note of every bird in that charmed and charming spot. It is interwoven with the poetry, the romance, and the history of the country in a sad story, which that pine-tree for fifty years commemorated, and then fell into decay. At last it bowed before the woodman's axe, in anticipation of being laid prone by some fierce storm.

The story of Jane M'Crea is an old, and oft-told tale, but there are always a new generation of readers who are interested in its repetition.

She was the young and lovely daughter of a Scotch clergyman in New Jersey. After his death she took up her abode with her brother, near Fort Edward. A neighbor's son became her accepted lover. The old war for independence was then raging. He was a loyalist, and was in the army of Burgoyne when, in the summer of 1777, it came sweeping victoriously from Lake Champlain to the Hudson. Jenny, as Miss M'Crea was called, visited a loyalist friend at Fort Edward, where she heard of the approach of the of the British, hoping to see her lover. But painted savages preceded the army. Early one morning a party of them rushed from the woods, seized Jenny and her friend, and started with them up the road toward Sandy Hill. Jenny was light and slender; her friend was a heavy, corpulent woman. The report of Indians near, soon reached the fort, and a detachment was sent out to confront them. The Indians were just making off with their prisoners, having Jenny on horseback, and her corpulent friend between two stalwart savages. The soldiers fired several volleys, but the Indians escaped unhurt. Not so the fair prisoner. A bullet intended for her captor killed the poor girl.

She fell to the ground near the spring, below the great pine-tree, and expired. The savages immediately scalped her, and carried her long black tresses in triumph to the camp of Burgoyne, to receive the usual reward for such trophies.

The bereaved lover purchased the beautiful locks of his betrothed, deserted from the army, and retired to Canada, where he lived to be an old man. He never recovered from the shock of that sad event. He had always been gay and garrulous; ever afterwards he was melancholy and taciturn. He never married; avoided society; and at the close of every July, near the time of the anniversary of his bereavement, he would shut himself in his room for several days, and refuse to see even his most intimate friends.

Such was the tragedy that caused the stately pine, to be called THE JANE M'CREA TREE.

The grave of Jane M'Crea may be seen in the Union Cemetery, at Fort Edward.

GLEN'S FALLS is an exceedingly pretty village. A very fine "Soldier's Monument" was erected here a year or two ago. The passage of the river here is through a rude ravine, in a mad descent of seventy-five feet, over a rocky precipice of nine hundred feet in length. In this vicinity were laid some of the scenes in Cooper's famous "Last of the Mohicans."

From Glen's Falls to Lake George is a fine ride of nine miles. Three coaches await the arrival of the train, and give promise of ample accommodation. Alas, for our expectations! All the passengers bound to Lake George are packed into and upon a single coach, until there is not an inch of room to spare, and trunks upon trunks are fastened behind. The drive to Caldwell is said to be charming—in scenery—and so it is; but if tourists are liable to be packed like sardines in a box, we recommend—until the railroad is extended—purchasing tickets to Glen's Falls only, and taking a private carriage thence to the Lake.

Within four miles of Lake George the road winds past a dark glen which conceals from view the Bloody Pond. Near it is a stern-looking old boulder, remembered in history as William's Rock. Here Colonel Williams was slain in 1775, in an engagement with the French and Indians. The hosts of the slain in this battle were cast into the waters, which have since been known by the name of Bloody Pond. It is now quiet enough, with the lily pads floating like emerald ornaments upon its bosom.

Our destination is Caldwell, and the scenery through which we pass, diversified by running streams, and ever changing landscapes of mountain, plain and valley, almost reconciles us to the dusty road, and to the fact that twelve passengers are inside the stage and nearly as many more on top.

Caldwell was for many years but a hamlet at the southern end of the lake. It is named from an eccentric gentleman—illiberal obstinacy is always posthumously beatified into eccentricity—who owned the whole region, built a hotel on the wrong spot, determined that no one else should build anywhere, and ardently desired that no more people should settle in the neighborhood; and in general, infested the southern shore with a success worthy of a mythological dragon.

Lake George is a mountain lake of extreme beauty, upon the verge of the wilderness. You ascend from its banks westward and plunge into a wild region. The hills that frame the water are low, and when not bare—for fires frequently consume many miles of woodland on the hillsides—are covered with the stifly outlined, dark and cold foliage of evergreens. Among these are no signs of life. You may well fancy the populace of the primeval forest yet

holding these retreats. You may well dream in the twilight that it were not impossible to catch the ring of a French or English rifle, or the wild whoop of an Indian; sure that the landscape you see, is the same that was seen by them and their remote ancestors.

Lake George is a strange lull in excitement after Saratoga. To be sure, there are gay belles here, and the prices at the Fort William Henry Hotel are equal to any in the land. Nevertheless its tranquillity is something like the morning after a ball. There is nothing but to croquet or sit on the piazza, or go boating or fishing upon the lake. It is a good place to study fancy fishermen who have taken their degrees in Wall street or Fifth Avenue. " Most of the visitors are guests of a day, but there are also pleasant parties—poets and painters often—who pass weeks at the lake or at one of the private houses near. These lovers of Lake George listen to enthusiastic stories of Saratoga as incredulously as to Syren-songs. To them Saratoga is but a name and a vapor, incredible as the fervor of a tropical day to the Russian Empress, in her icy palace. These are parties of a character rare in our country, who do not utterly surrender the summer to luxurious idleness, but steal honey from the flowers as they fly." This tribute to those who

"Come early, and linger late"

upon the shores of Lake George, is uttered by George William Curtis who "never says a thing amiss," and its justice will be recognized by all who have themselves, been more than the guests of a day. The Indian name for Lake George was Horicon. It is far more melodious than its prosaic modern name.

Here Fort William Henry, upon the southern shore of Lake George, once guarded the possessions of England—while Carillon or Ticonderoga upon Lake Champlain secured the dominion of France in the magnificent province of Canada, which was justly regarded as the most illustrious jewel of the French empire.

" These two forts," says a recent historical writer, " stand venerable in their ruins at either gateway of Lake George, monuments of a heroic age and of the wrestlings of giants for the possession of a continent. To-day the shores of Horicon furnish fashionable resorts for the refined or the curious, who bask away the summer hours, perhaps careless or ignorant of the great events which once transpired beneath their feet or within their vision. Yet the possession of these places has engaged the attention of Kings, Cabinets and Parliaments. The best blood of great nations has been freely spent, and millions of treasure lavished, for their conquest and defence.

"Armies have crossed the ocean, tribes of red men have been marshalled by civilized genius, rival and foreign flags have all met here. Carnage, the butchery of the tomahawk, the wasting of a siege, the wretchedness of woman have all been known. The feast of human flesh has been prepared, and the soft voice of the Jesuit Priest heard here.

" Protestant and Catholic, English and French, white and red men, the cannon and the scalping knife, extremes the most opposite, passions the most violent, have met, and struggled *here* for the mastery.

"All, all are gone now. From out the ashes a third power has arisen, to which the Red Cross of England and the Lily of France are alike indifferent. From mountain to mountain, the American Eagle utters the scream of LIBERTY."

Fort William Henry Hotel stands upon the site of the old fort of that name. It is a fine excursion by the steamer Minnehaha to the landing near the village of Ticonderoga, four miles from the venerable ruins of Fort Ticonderoga on Lake Champlain. Parties can go and return in one day.

Lake George is thirty-six miles in length. Its boat-boys count its islands by the days of the year, and tell you of three hundred and sixty-five. It is a story agreeable enough to hear the first time, but rather wearisome ere it falls on your ear for the *last* time.

Diamond Isle, Long Island and Doom, or Fourteen Mile Island, are the most noticeable of the islands. By the way, somebody counted last year, and declares that Lake George has really only two hundred and ninety-five of these little bits of land which rise up fresh, green and, as it were, *clean-cut* from out of the transparent depths; some quite large, others mere dots, but every one beautiful. The towering peaks of the Black Mountains encircle the lake, their wild heights rendering the landscape most picturesque.

Excursions are made from Caldwell daily in the trim Ganouskie —a saucy little craft built on the lake. One of the best of these trips is to Northwest Bay, to Bolton Landing, and to Trout Pavilion, four miles from Bolton. The best fishing in the lake is to be found here.

Upon the east side of the bay, Tongue Mountain comes in, literally, into the lake. Passing Tongue Mountain, we enter the Narrows at the base of the loftiest and boldest heights which environ Lake George. The water is here four hundred feet deep, and wonderfully clear and sparkling.

While at Ticonderoga, *we*, however, will avail ourselves of a roomy and comfortable stage, and ride over a rough and romantic road to Fort Ticonderoga.

It appears to be a part of the regular programme, when in sight of "Old Fort Ti," for the agent of the route, mounted on the wheel of one coach, to deliver a pithy little address, which causes great merriment, while the passengers gaze at the ruins.

By this route we follow the wild and joyous course by which Horicon reaches Lake Champlain. Bold rapids and striking cascades characterize its passage.

Lake Champlain lies between Vermont and New York. It is ninety miles in length, and its width varies from one-fourth of a mile to fourteen miles.

The steamers upon Lake Champlain are very elegant and commodious, but an excursion upon its waters forms a curious contrast to the trip on Lake George. The scenery is fine; the Green Mountains appear in the distance on the left, the Black range on the right; rugged cliffs sometimes loom up on either side, and then low, irregular border-lines appear; but the water has none of that peculiar clearness which marks the other lake. Flags, rushes, trees and bushes grow up lawlessly in the very midst of it—all the more noticeable after one has just viewed the chiseled borders of that silvery sheet which in olden times was called "Horicon."

Ticonderoga was the first stronghold taken by us from the British in the Revolution. Here Ethan Allen with his Green Mountain Boys penetrated to the very bedside of the English Commander and demanded his surrender.

"In whose name and to whom?" demanded the astonished officer.

"In the name of the Great Jehovah and the Continental Congress," thundered the intrepid Allen, and the fort was surrendered.

Mount Independence lies in Vermont, opposite Ticonderoga, about one mile distant.

TICONDEROGA LAKE CHAMPLAIN.

Crown Point is the site of old Fort St. Frederick, erected by the French in 1731. It was Lord Pitt who ordered in 1758, upon its capture by the English, that Fort St. Frederick should be rebuilt and enlarged, and known in the future as Crown Point.

Although never completed, this fort is said to have cost the English government more than two million of pounds sterling. The ramparts were about twenty-five feet thick and nearly the same in height and were built of solid masonry. The whole circuit was nearly nine hundred yards. A broad ditch surrounded the work. On the north was a gate and from the northeast bastion a covered way leading to the water. But the glory of Crown Point has departed.

Passing on beyond Port Henry and West Port, we reach Port Kent, sixty-six miles from Ticonderoga, ninety miles from Whitehall, three hundred and thirteen from New York, and are now at what is generally considered *one of the very best gates*, by which the Tourist may enter the Adirondacks.

We doubt if any one, bound for the wilderness,—with the delightful prospect of camping out before them, and with new fishing rods, and "flies" amid their baggage, which they long to make trial of, as the school boy who has had his jack-knife confiscated by the teacher, longs for recess and its restoration—*can* truly *enjoy* this trip after Lake George is left behind, and ere the Adirondacks are entered. It may be pleasant and interesting to view the scenery upon the shores of Lake Champlain, but who will drink cold tea with zest, when a more cheering draught may be in a little time secured?

Do not be affronted, ye who love the green shores and placid waters of Lake Champlain, by this comparison, which may seem to you so ill chosen! We mean simply to imply, that, with the excitement of a prospective trip to the Adirondack region, thrilling through the monotone of everyday life—more quiet joys seem tame in comparison with those which are promised by fancy and imagination.

And now, gracious reader, before we enter the wilderness—we assume that you *are* gracious, because you have thus far borne us company—let a word be said in your ear respecting the guise in which you are invited to journey over a tract of country as large as the whole State of Connecticut, and the experiences which await you there.

An enthusiast says, that none should visit the wilderness who have not dreamed of the trip as prisoners dream of freedom! A more prosaic person advises " those who love good fishing, clear, fresh air, and delightful scenery, and honest sport, to visit the Adirondack region. But if a man trembles at the song of a mosquito, or the sight of a black fly, or if he looks upon a visit to the country as a business investment which will not pay unless he catches so many fish for so many dollars, he had better put a pin-hook on a piece of cord, and fish in his cistern."

It is our own opinion, dear reader, that if you have never been a " Tom-Boy," either male or female, at some period in your career—that you will never be of those who find the Adirondacks truly enjoyable. If walnut furniture and spring beds are essential to your comfort, you must look for comfort elsewhere, and *especially* if you are one of the critics of that much abused volume, " Murray's Adventures in the Wilderness "—we entreat you not to go thither.

And here let us say one word in defense of that " sensation " book, as it has been termed by hosts who were decoyed by its fascinating pages into following Mr. Murray's track. The wild breath of the wild woods pervades that volume. It is written by one who loves nature in her most primitive array—who loves sport well enough to sacrifice for it all those advantages which money will buy at Newport or Saratoga or Long Branch—will buy almost anywhere *except* in the wilderness. The wilderness *to him* was all that he represented it—to many "solid" men who cannot exist without their morning paper and the city's hum and the postman's call—to ladies who *must* have white morning wrappers, point lace shawls and Saratoga trunks—the Adirondack region is indeed a *waste and howling "Wilderness."*

The daily life and the geography of that region are alike but little known. A vague notion that the Adirondacks mean North Elba, and that North Elba means John Brown's home, pervades the mind of the city dame.

The city *man* has visions of deer—herds of them within *very* easy rifle range.

Possibly these good people ought not to be criticised for their lack of information, when even *Appleton's Handbook of American Travel for* 1871 *makes such very slight mention* of the Adirondack Company's railroad, which is projected from Saratoga Springs to Ogdensburgh, on the St. Lawrence river, passing through the very heart of the Adirondack region. This road is already completed to a point forty-nine miles distant from Saratoga, and five miles beyond the "Glen." Work upon it is rapidly progressing. Of this route, we shall speak anon.

There are five parallel mountain ranges known under the general name of the Adirondacks, which traverse this portion of the State in a northeasterly direction, terminating either at Lake Champlain or in the plains of Canada.

The Adirondacks are really the eastern range only, but the term is usually applied to all. Some of the mountains are well known by name, as Whiteface, and Tahawas, which signifies in Indian dialect, " He splits the sky."

The mountain region is upwards of one hundred miles in diameter. It is estimated that one thousand lakes, many of them as yet unvisited, lie embedded in this vast forest of pine and hemlock. Sixty-four lakes, ponds and rivers are said to be visible, without a glass, from the summit of Whiteface.

Between two of the highest of the Adirondack Mountains, at the bottom of a crevice a thousand feet or more in depth, precipice-walled and gloomy, lies Avalanche Lake, two thousand nine hundred feet above tide-level. It is surmised by many, that this lake and Lake Colden, at the south of it, were once one sheet, or at least connected by a deep ravine. A slide, rolled down from Mount Colden, closed the channel, threw back the waters, and the lake, avalanche born, was formed. Last August, a furious storm of wind and rain occurred among the Adirondacks. A visitor reports, that during that storm a mighty avalanche rushed down the side of Mount Colden, falling into Lake Avalanche, and literally making a dam across it, and dividing it into two lakes. Amidst many difficulties, he visited the wild spot soon after this occurrence, while yet the dark waters were muddy from recent disturbances, and the lake strewn with floating timber. It is predicted, that after a few more mountain slides, Avalanche Lake will become Avalanche Pass.

Telegraph lines now extend to the Adirondack region, and telegraph offices will be found at the principal hotels.

A few years hence, and but a *flavor* of forest life will linger around localities which are now little changed from the primeval forest.

PRINCESS NOMENA.
See Chapter 14.

THE NEW YORK
PUBLIC LIBRARY

ASTOR, LENOX AND
TILDEN FOUNDATIONS
R L

The John Brown Tract is in the southerly and least interesting portion of the North Woods. Yet the way thither from Keeseville leads through the Wilmington Notch, a famous mountain pass, and enables those who choose, to climb grand old Whiteface.

Port Kent is near the mouth of the Au Sable river, which, between Port Kent and Keeseville, passes through a wonderful chasm, forming what are known as the Walled Banks of the Au Sable river. The river plunges in hot haste over a precipice—Birmingham Falls—seventy feet in height, and rushes for a distance of two miles through a chasm which is in many places one hundred and thirty feet deep—and again it is forced through a channel only a few feet in width.

In 1859, while John Brown was on trial for his life at Harper's Ferry—when some were calling him " madman," while some said " saint "—a visitor to his desolate home thus recorded his impressions:

" The traveler into the enchanted land of the Adirondacks has his choice of two routes from Keeseville to the lower Saranac Lake. The one least frequented, and most difficult, has the grandest mountain pass that the State can show. After driving over twenty-two miles of mountain road, from Keeseville, past wild summits bristling with stumps, and the villages where every other man is black from the iron foundry, and every alternate one black from the charcoal pit, your pathway makes a turn at the little hamlet of Wilmington, and you find yourself facing a wall of mountain, with only glimpses of the one, wild gap which you must penetrate. In two miles more you have passed the last house this side the Notch, and then drive on over a rugged way, with no companion but the stream which ripples and roars below.

" Soon the last charcoal clearing is passed, thick woods of cedar and birch close around you—Whiteface, the high mountain on your right, comes nearer and nearer, and close upon your left are glimpses of a wall, black and bare as iron, rising sheer for four hundred feet above your head. Coming from the soft marble country of Vermont, or the pale granite of Massachusetts, there seems something weird and forbidding in this utter blackness.

"On your left, the giant wall now appears nearer, now retreats again; on your right foams the merry stream, breaking into graceful cascades—and across it the great mountain Whiteface, seamed with slides. Now the woods upon your left are displaced by the iron wall, almost touching the roadside; against its steep abruptness scarcely a shrub can cling, scarcely a fern flutter; it takes your breath away, but five miles of perilous driving conduct you through it, and beyond this stern passway, this cave of iron, lie the lovely lakes and mountains of the Adirondacks, and the homestead of John Brown.

"The Notch seems beyond the world. North Elba and its dozen houses is beyond the Notch, and there is a wilder little mountain road, which seems to rise beyond North Elba. But the house we seek is not even on that road, but behind it and beyond it—you ride a mile or two—take down a pair of bars—beyond the bars faith takes you across a half-cleared field, and you come out on a clearing—there is a little frame house, unpainted, set in a girdle of black stumps, with all heaven about it for a wider girdle—on a high hillside—forests on the north and west—the glorious line of the Adirondacks on the east, and on the south, one slender road leading off to Westport—a road so straight, that you could sight a United States marshal on it for five miles."

This was John Brown's home in 1859. But he had a wider perspective than the Adirondacks, a perspective which embraced *universal freedom.*

Now the stages which run from Keeseville to the lower Saranac Lake pass the deserted homestead of John Brown, with its granite boulder, and his grave close by.

The Indian Pass in which the Hudson has its birth, may be visited about seven miles north of North Elba.

There are comfortable hotels at the Lower Saranac, and the traveler will find that many beside himself have been impelled in spirit to come hither.

At this point Guides can be hired, and excursions planned, to almost any desirable spot for sport. Fine scenery can be found elsewhere—sport, rare sport, *cannot*.

The trips are made in long slender boats which admit the carrying of but very little baggage.

Deer are growing more plentiful in the woods—thanks to the Game Laws—but they are also growing *wise*. They know a rifle afar, and, always wary of their enemy man, by instinct, they are also growing more so by education. But there are boat-loads of glorious fish within the streams; there are guides who are uncut diamonds, and *also* guides who are like paste diamonds, with the addition of an edge which will cut *you*. The only point upon which the generality of travelers will not agree with Mr. Murray, is that concerning the black fly. He calls it a myth—*almost*. If this be so, may the saints preserve us from encountering the black fly in reality—*cry the bitten*.

In " Hints for Travelers," in one of the chapters of this volume, an account is given of the best method or methods of managing this enemy. He is a formidable one to most people.

To enjoy " camping out " to perfection, try it upon the southern or western shore of Raquette Lake. You will find the lower Saranac region an " old camp ground " in comparison.

From the Lower Saranac, *the* excursion seems to be to the Upper Saranac Lakes. There are about a dozen in number. Above these lies the great St. Regis Lake.

The whole region is rich in its charms for those *only* who love nature better than fashion, and who can " rough it " a little for the sake of health and sport.

From the Saranac region our way lies to Lake Pleasant by intermediate waters and portages. A portage is a " carry " where the tune in vogue is not " paddle your own canoe," but " carry your own canoe." Truly, if you have been there, you will *know how it is yourself!*

From Lake Pleasant a stage ride of thirty miles brings us to the quiet town of Amsterdam upon the New York Central road, from whence we can go west, or return to Albany.

The routes are legion. From Plattsburg by railway to Au Sable station, opposite Point of Rocks ten miles above Keeseville, gives the shortest stage ride.

By Lake Champlain and Port Kent to Keeseville, is also a favorite route.

From Crown Point to Long Lake by stage, and thence by water to the Saranac Lakes, is another mode of approach.

From Utica to Booneville, and thence by stage, is another. By Central railroad to Amsterdam, and thence by stage, numbers one more route.

From Saratoga to a point five miles beyond the Glen, lands the traveler in a fine vicinity for sport, but the heart of the woods is not yet reached, nor the *best* sport attainable.

Reader we wish for you, upon either of these trips—your heart's desire, whatever it be—health, and *no* mosquito bites!

"THE POOL WHERE THE BIG TROUT LIE."

X.

THE New York Central road traverses the entire length of the Empire State from east to west. It has two termini at the eastern end, one at Albany and the other at Troy, the branches uniting, after seventeen miles, at Schenectady.

It then continues in one line to Syracuse, one hundred and forty-eight miles from Albany, when it has again a double route as far as Rochester—one route being known as the "main," and the other as the "old line," or Auburn road.

SCHENECTADY is not a place of much interest to the traveler, although it is one of the oldest towns in the State, and is distinguished as the seat of Union College, founded in 1795, and rendered illustrious by the long Presidency of Dr. Nott, whose sermon at Albany against dueling, occasioned by the death of Alexander Hamilton, is claimed as the greatest oratorical effort, of the early part of this century.

Schenectady was established as a trading post with the Indians as early as 1620. It suffered as frontier towns invariably do, and was visited with massacre and fire in 1690, and again the tomahawk was raised during the French and Indian war.

Leaving Schenectady, the railroad trains cross the Mohawk river and the Erie canal upon a bridge nearly *one thousand* feet in length.

At PALATINE BRIDGE the stage may be taken to Sharon Springs, which is but ten miles distant, over a good plank road.

From FORT PLAIN, the next station, a regular line of stages run to Cherry Valley and Cooperstown. In the vicinity is old Fort Plain, of Revolutionary memory.

At LITTLE FALLS may be seen perhaps the most wild and picturesque scenery upon this route. Here, there is a bold passage of the Mohawk river and the Erie canal through a rocky defile, which affords a view of great beauty.

Fifty years ago a noted stage route from Rochester to Albany led through Little Falls. The road wound along near a precipice by the river side. On one occasion, General Winfield Scott was in the stage, when at a sharp turn near the bottom of the hill, a Pennsylvania wagon was seen winding its way up diagonally. The driver saw but one escape from a disastrous collision, and that, to most persons, would have appeared even more dangerous than the collision. However, having no time for reflection, he instantly guided his team over the precipice and into the river, from which the horses, passengers, coach and all were safely extricated. The passengers, following General Scott's example made the driver a handsome present as a reward for his courage and sagacity.

Near the ancient village of HERKIMER, lie the fertile and celebrated German Flats, nearly a thousand acres of which were once owned by two parties, Judge Weaver and Colonel Bellinger. These two splendid farms have long since, by a very common pro-

AQUEDUCT AT LITTLE FALLS.

cess, been melted into one. General C. P. Bellinger married the daughter of Judge Weaver, and thus inherited both farms.

UTICA, ninety-five miles from Albany, is a handsome city upon the south bank of the Mohawk river. Its manufactures interest one class of visitors to the city—the State Lunatic Asylum call some here upon sad errands—while many summer travelers, here take the Utica and Black River railway, by which Trenton Falls are reached.

The large woolen mills of Mr. A. T. Stewart are located here, and we rejoice to chronicle an act of beneficence which has not we believe been mentioned by the papers.

During the severe weather of last winter, Mr. Stewart was informed by his agent in Utica that the mills had five hundred tons of coal to spare, which might be sold to advantage, as coal was scarce and prices high. Mr. Stewart replied, "Sell none; but, as the price is high and the article scarce, give away the whole to the working people of the mills—share and share alike;" which was accordingly done.

Anthony Trollope, the celebrated English novelist, who has written a book on "North America," says, that "a general air of fat prosperity pervades all the towns between Albany and Buffalo, and this air is quite as strong at Utica as anywhere else."

Trenton Falls was described by N. P. Willis as "the most enjoyably beautiful spot among the resorts of romantic scenery in our country." As Mr. Willis spent a good deal of time there, making himself familiar with every feature of the locality, and become devotedly attached to the place, *all* visitors may not be inclined to agree with him in ranking Trenton Falls *above* all other romantic resorts. But the tourist should not fail, in some of his summer trips, to obtain a view of the wonderful chasm which the foaming torrent of waters has there made.

Trenton Falls is about an hour's ride from Utica. There is a good hotel at the Falls, kept by the owner of the property. The internal arrangements are pleasant and home-like. The parlors are adorned with fine paintings and engravings, the music-room contains a pipe-organ, and, what will be appreciated by many, there is no occasion for any elaborate display of toilettes.

Behind the hotel a winding path through a grove leads the visitor to a steep staircase; and descending this he finds himself in a magnificent ravine, through which the amber-colored waters foam and dash. The name of the river is Canada Creek West; but, as that is hardly euphonious, the course of water which forms the Falls has been called after the town. This water course is nearly two miles in length, and along the space of these two miles it is impossible to say where the greatest beauty exists.

To see Trenton aright, one must be careful not to have too much water. A sufficiency is no doubt desirable, and it may be, that at the close of summer, before the autumnal rains have fallen, there may occasionally be an insufficiency. But if there be too much, the passage up the rock, along the river is impossible. The way on which the tourist should walk becomes the bed of the stream, and the great charm of the place cannot be enjoyed.

That charm consists in descending into the ravine of the river, down amidst the rocks through which it has cut its channel, and in walking up the bed against the stream, in climbing the sides of the various Falls, and sticking close to the river till an envious blockade is reached, which comes sheer down into the water, and prevents further progress. This is nearly two miles above the steps by which the descent is made; and every foot of this distance is

TRENTON FALLS.

NEW YORK
PUBLIC LIBRARY

ASTOR, LENOX AND
TILDEN FOUNDATIONS

wildly beautiful. When the river is very low, there is a pathway even beyond this block; but when this is the case, there can hardly be water enough to make the Fall satisfactory.

There is no one special cataract at Trenton which is in itself either wonderful or pre-eminently beautiful. It is the position, form, color and rapidity of the river which gives the charm. It runs through a deep ravine, the sides of which rise sometimes with the sharpness of the walls of a stone sarcophagus. They are rounded, too, towards the bed, as is the bottom of a sarcophagus. Along the side of the right bank of the river, there is a passage, which when the freshets come is altogether covered. This passage is sometimes very narrow, but in the narrowest parts an iron chain is affixed to the rock. It is slippery and wet, and it is well for ladies, when visiting the place, to be provided with rubber shoes, which keep a hold upon the stone.

There are two actual cataracts—one not far above the steps by which the descent is made into the channel, and the other close under a summer-house, near to which the visitors reascend into the wood. But these cataracts, though by no means despicable as cataracts, leave comparatively a slight impression. They tumble down with sufficient violence, and the usual fantastic disposition of their forces; but as cataracts within a day's journey of NIAGARA, they would be nothing.

Up beyond the summer-house, the passage along the river can be continued for another mile, but it is rough, and the climbing in some places difficult, yet the succession of rapids, and the twisting of the channels, and the forms of the rocks, are as wild and beautiful as the imagination can desire.

The banks of the river are closely wooded on each side; and though this circumstance does not at first seem to add much to the beauty, seeing that the ravine is so deep, that the absence of wood above would hardly be noticed, still there are broken clefts ever and anon, through which the colors of the foliage show themselves, and straggling boughs and rough roots break through the rocks here and there, and add to the wildness and charm of the whole.

The walk back from the summer-house through the wood is very lovely; but it would be a disappointing walk to visitors who had been prevented by a flood in the river from coming up the channel, for it indicates plainly how requisite it is that the river should be seen from below and not from above. The best view of the larger Fall itself, is that seen from the wood.

We present amid our pages three views, which will be recognized by all who are conversant with the aspect of the different Falls at Trenton.

In conclusion, we will only say, in regard to Trenton, that tourists from New York frequently visit Trenton Falls and Niagara in the same trip—taking, perhaps, on one way, the Erie, and on the other, the Central railway. We advise visiting Trenton Falls *first*—Niagara Falls can be compared to nothing else, it stands alone—and the picturesque beauty of Trenton, in its wild, rocky bed, is better appreciated when the impression of Niagara is not fresh on the mind.

The John Brown Tract of the Adirondacks may be reached by continuing upon the Black River railway beyond Trenton to Booneville, eighteen miles distant.

Returning to Utica, we pass ROME, VERONA, ONEIDA and CHITTENANGO, upon our way to SYRACUSE.

At Verona and Chittenango are springs of considerable note. The medicinal qualities of the Chittenango waters are very

AT TRENTON FALLS.

similar in character to those of the celebrated White Sulphur Springs in Virginia, and seem to possess their wonderful healing powers, especially in cutaneous affections and diseases of the liver, stomach and bowels, and other functions. But these waters, like all that contain sulphuretted hydrogen gas, appear to have a deleterious effect upon pulmonary complaints, and should be avoided by those who are thus afflicted. For that reason they are also admirable tests by which to discover a *real* pulmonary disease, the symptoms of which other disorders sometimes assume.

SYRACUSE is a marvel in the suddenness and rapidity of its growth. In 1811, it was a tangled and almost impenetrable swamp, thickly inhabited by frogs and water-snakes. Upon the locality over which Syracuse now extends, there was, in the year to which we refer, but one human habitation; that was Cossett's Tavern, near the site of the present Syracuse House.

It is an *on dit* at the present time in Syracuse society, that one of its belles, who has been some time abroad, was recently married in Europe to a Russian gentleman. It was, of course, after the ceremonial of the Greek church; and there is so much that is picturesque about the pageant—what with the blue velvet and silver-laced robe of the priest, the holding of heavy silver crowns over the heads of the happy pair, for the priest takes the united hands of the two in his, and marches with them slowly three times around his altar; all the while the groomsmen follow, holding the silver crowns over the heads of bride and bridegroom. These crowns are so heavy that some of the assistants frequently come to aid the groomsmen. Praying and chanting is liberally mingled with the performance, and three times they take the sacrament. The bride and bridegroom have a piece of rose-colored satin to stand upon, and there is a vulgar belief that the one who treads first upon the satin will hold the upper hand in the household. Upon this occasion the bridegroom gracefully placed the beautiful bride first upon the pink rug.

The most extensive salt manufactories in the country, are to be found here. The land containing the Saline Springs, is owned by the State, and is leased free of rent, to be used, however, only in this manufacture. The wells are dug, and the water pumped, at the expense of the State, and the manufacturer pays a duty of one cent per bushel.

Fine salt is prepared by boiling, while coarse salt is made by solar evaporation.

An experiment has been made, by order of the Secretary of War, to examine into the relative merits of the Onondaga and Turks Island salts, and it has been proven, that home manufacture is equal, if not superior, to foreign.

Syracuse is connected with Binghamton by railway, and also with Oswego.

The best time ever made in this country by any railroad train, was recorded here last summer, when Mr. William Vanderbilt (a son of Cornelius, the mariner), and certain directors of the New York Central railway, were conveyed from Rochester to Syracuse, eighty-one miles, in sixty-one minutes.

Between Syracuse and Rochester, upon the "main line," are seven flourishing towns. We shall, however, find more that is of interest to the traveler by following the "old line," or Auburn road, to Rochester.

We are now in the "lake" country of western New York, of which comparatively very little is known. There are towns in this lake region which are *lovely resorts* in summer, but in winter, rain and fog, and clouds and snow prevail to such an extent, that the sun is not seen a dozen times in a month.

At the head of Skaneateles Lake was at one time a Water Cure, lying in a valley with such a range of rocky summits upon the west, that the sun set for the denizens of the " Cure " at three P. M. in summer, and not long after *noon* upon winter days.

AUBURN is delightfully situated near Owasco Lake, which is twelve miles in length. The State Prison is here. Auburn is also noted for its Theological Seminary. Thus extremes meet. Auburn is also known as the home of Hon. William H. Seward. It has many fine residences, and a highly cultivated society.

CAYUGA is the point where the railroad crosses Cayuga Lake by a bridge over a mile in length. The cars should be left at this point, if the Tourist desires to see Taghkanic Falls, which Dr. Cheever pronounces " the Staubbach of Switzerland most absolutely reproduced, and of concentrated beauty and grandeur."

Taking the boat up Cayuga Lake (*south*), and reluctantly learning to say *up*, when inclination prompts us to say *down*, we notice SPRINGPORT, the first landing, where Napoleon Third lived for some time while in this country.

The next stopping place, AURORA, claims the honor of being the prettiest town in the country. Here resides Mr. Henry Wells, the founder of the American Merchants' Union Express Company.

At Frog Point, or Trumansburg, we leave the boat and enter a stage which runs to the Taghkanic House, just in front of Taghkanic Falls, the highest in New York State. Truly you think that never was stage fare—a quarter—better earned than when the steep hill, one mile long, is climbed which brings you to your destination.

Taghkanic Creek flows through a rich and flourishing country, till it reaches a point less than two miles distant from Cayuga Lake, where a rocky ledge rises some fifty or sixty feet directly in its bed. But the stream has been inspired to excavate for itself a channel from one hundred to four hundred feet in depth, and four hundred feet across at its lower extremity. Through this chasm the waters hurry on to the precipice, whence they fall into a rocky basin.

At the bottom of the fall, the ravine is upward of four hundred feet in perpendicular height, and the waters form a cataract more than fifty feet higher than that at Niagara.

ITHACA lies at the head of Cayuga Lake, and can be reached not only by steamboat from Cayuga, but by the Cayuga division of the Erie railway.

In the immediate vicinity of Ithaca are fifteen waterfalls—some of them being really very beautiful. It is, however, more noted as the seat of the Cornell University.

The Cornell University originated in the combined bounty of the United States Government and of the Honorable Ezra Cornell. In 1862, Congress passed an act granting public lands to the several States and Territories which might provide Colleges for the benefit of Agriculture and the Mechanic Arts.

The share of the State of New York was in land scrip, representing nine hundred and ninety thousand acres. From the first, the State determined to concentrate this fund in a single institution worthy of the Commonwealth.

In 1865, the entire proceeds of the land grant were transferred to the Cornell University upon its compliance with certain conditions, of which the most important were that Ezra Cornell should

TRENTON FALLS.

give to the Institution five hundred thousand dollars, and that provision should be made for the education, free of all charge for tuition, of one student from each Assembly district of the State. At the first meeting of the Trustees thereafter, Mr. Cornell fulfilled the requirements of the Charter. He then made the additional gift of over two hundred acres of land, with buildings, as a farm to be attached to the College of Agriculture, and of the Jewett collection in Geology and Palæontology—a collection which had cost him ten thousand dollars; and he has given since that time, other gifts to the amount of twenty-five thousand dollars. Besides this, he has expended about two hundred thousand dollars in purchasing the land scrip and locating the lands of the University.

The career of the Institution since that period has been one of constant advancement. The interest of the public has never ceased to manifest itself. Gifts of various kinds—collections, sums for building purposes, machinery and models—have been freely bestowed upon the University. The value of these gifts is estimated at nearly four hundred thousand dollars.

During the three years which have elapsed since its doors were first thrown open, the number of instructors has increased from twenty-four to almost forty. Two additional edifices of stone have been erected, and another has been commenced. A large temporary building of wood, for laboratory purposes, has been constructed. Roads have been laid out and bridges built. Thirty thousand volumes have been added to the library. A University printing-office, on a large scale, has been established. A cabinet of American birds, a cabinet of cereals, an extensive herbarium, a cabinet of botanical models, a cabinet of anatomical models, have, among other collections, increased the treasures of the various museums The facilities for instruction have thus kept pace with the increase in the number of undergraduates, which has more than doubled since 1868. The sums paid for manual and other labor to such of these as needed the assistance, has exceeded twenty thousand dollars.

In 1869, the following paragraph went the rounds of the newspapers: "Cornell University has its first ' Freshwoman,' Miss Jennie Spencer, who has been admitted to the Freshman class after having passed an excellent examination." And in the fall of 1870 nearly three hundred new pupils were received, involving the appointment of four new professors, among whom was Mr. O. P. Cornell, a son of the founder.

Professor Goldwin Smith and Professor Fiske have lately selected the site for a large residence in Ithaca. The dwelling will be a large double house, planned and built to suit the taste and convenience of these bachelor professors. It will cost about twelve thousand dollars. Professor Smith is said to be a gentleman of fortune, and can afford to build as he pleases, but it is to be hoped that he will avoid that bad style of architecture so popular in the United States, the " pointed Ironic."

The chimes which summon its students to their morning duties were presented to the University by Miss M'Graw, whose father, Mr. John M'Graw, has recently announced to the authorities his intention to erect a library building at a cost of fifty thousand dollars. The new structure is to stand between the two main University edifices, is to be built like them, in the Florentine palatial style of architecture, of white and dark blue stone, and to include a lofty campanile, in which the M'Graw chimes are to be placed.

Mr. Hiram Sibley, of Rochester, is also erecting a large stone edifice for the use of the College of the Mechanic Arts.

Mr. Greene Smith, of Geneva, the only son of Gerrit Smith, who is an ardent naturalist, has bestowed upon the Museum of Geology his costly collection of American birds, and is still constantly increasing it.

With all these endowments, Cornell University is, and cannot fail to be, in a steadily increasing degree, a "power in the land."

A Horticultural School for young Ladies, has been projected at Ithaca, with the object of giving an industrial, as well as a literary education.

The industrial instruction will not be confined to horticulture, but will be extended to such other branches of business as women can appropriately carry on. A generous grant of land has been made by the Hon. Ezra Cornell, and the success of this enterprise is confidently predicted.

Returning from Ithaca to Cayuga, we proceed by rail to the next station, SENECA FALLS, beyond which is GENEVA, a fair and flourishing city, the seat of Hobart College, of the Medical Institute of Geneva College, and of the Geneva Union School.

The site of Geneva is admirably chosen, upon the banks of Seneca, which is one of the most interesting and beautiful lakes of Western New York. It is very deep and never freezes over. Steamboats run between Jefferson at the south end of the lake, and Geneva at the north end.

WATKINS GLEN, is situated at the southern extremity of Seneca Lake. A daily line of steamboats from Geneva, renders this place accessible to those who travel by the New York Central route—while it is also approached by railway from Elmira, by tourists who come by the Erie road from the east, or by the Williamsport and Elmira railway from Pennsylvania.

It will undoubtedly surprise many travelers to learn the fact, that over *sixty thousand* names were registered upon the hotel books at Watkins, last summer.

The best description thus far given of the Glen is, that it "*reminds one of the Mammoth Cave, with the lid lifted off!*" The Glen was considered by Secretary Seward, of such interest, that he brought the whole Diplomatic Corps to visit it, on the occasion of that tour in which he showed them some of the wonders of our country.

The Glen is really a rift or gorge in a rocky bluff, some six hundred feet in height. It opens abruptly upon Franklin, the principal street in the village. First entering a huge amphitheatre, to which there is no apparent exit, the visitor looks up at rocks towering above his head—then follows the path to the western end, where the walls of rock overlap each other, leaving a narrow passage, through and up which he passes by a steep stair-way to the *First Glen.*

Here it is always cool. The overhanging rocks are crowned with a fringe of trees, through which the sunlight is seldom seen. At the upper end of this half-mile Glen, is a waterfall some seventy or eighty feet in height. Ascending a stair-case, which is well nigh a ladder, we reach the Mountain House, as it is called. Then follow three more Glens, with their wild and picturesque beauties.

The crowning attraction of the fourth Glen, is the Rainbow Fall, behind which the path winds along. The four "Glens" spread over some three miles of space.

In this vicinity there are other glens and waterfalls, of themselves well worthy the attention of the tourist. Their wonders and beauties are second only to the Glen at Watkins.

There are pleasant drives through a country dotted with neat villages, blooming with orchards and vineyards, abounding in all agreeable and picturesque objects; but says a recent visitor, the genial Porte Crayon:—We returned to the Glen day after day, and found that, instead of palling, its weird charms rather grew upon us. At each visit some new beauty was developed, some curious nook or angle, unremarked before, arrested our attention; and we took leave regretfully, impressed with the belief that we had not seen half of its wonders.

In conclusion, we would commend the spot to some of our great landscape artists, as promising subjects worthy of their powers. To the invalid there is no more healthful or invigorating resort. To complete its claims to their regard, there is now in process of erection a large and convenient sanitarium, where the malingering public may be dosed with pure air, exercise, and cheerful recreation—nature's medicines—on scientific principles.

If any one doubts the superior healthfulness of this region, let him visit our ancient friend, Thomas Terryberry, who lives at the head of the Glen. This patriarch, still brisk and merry as a cricket, alert on his feet as a boy, with all his faculties clear and sound, boasts that he is ninety-seven years of age. Now, as we have the best local authority for asserting that he has been ninety-seven for the last sixteen years, we may safely predict that he can live sixteen years longer without getting much ahead of "his century."

No place is more easy of access than Watkins, located directly on the great line of travel to and from Niagara, of which the Glen is a worthy pendant; and any modern Dr. Syntax, philosophically curious in sight-seeing, may have the opportunity to decide whether it is more enjoyable to take one's quantum of sublimity in one stunning, foaming gulp, or to sip it more coolly and luxuriously through a spindling tunnel three miles in length.

From Watkins' Glen we return to Geneva, and go to CLIFTON SPRINGS. There is here an eminent Water Cure establishment, and the water of the Springs is esteemed by many a beverage fit to be borne among the immortals by Ganymedes.

The Clifton Spa House was erected as a dispensary in 1806, when the springs, then gushing out on the borders of a rough marsh and tangled forest, were visited by invalids from the surrounding country. For fifty years these waters have been famous for their cure of bilious and cutaneous disorders; and yet it is only about a dozen years that they have been much known beyond the region of Central New York.

Below the beautiful grove of maple, basswood, ash and chestnut trees, through which the visitors stroll to the fountains, there is a pretty lake, with an island in its centre, planted with shrubbery and adorned with a pavilion.

From Clifton Springs to CANANDAIGUA is a pleasant ride of eleven or twelve miles. This is a beautiful town at the north end of Canandaigua Lake. And next we steam into Rochester, twenty-nine miles distant.

ROCHESTER is noted for its enterprise—it is noted also for the number of its beautiful homes. In comparison with its population, it covers more ground than almost any other city in the Union.

Considering Brooklyn as an adjunct to New York, Rochester now ranks in the scale of population and business as the third city in the Union.

The city dates back to the erection of a saw-mill upon the east side of the river, in 1808, but there was no recognized community till three or four years later.

Rochester—favored city—lies in the heart of the Genesee country, the Garden of the Empire State.

To a large extent, New England influences and ancestry have moulded character and society here, and transmitted that indomitable energy which has made Rochester the beautiful home of a refined and wealthy people.

Its name is derived from Colonel Nathaniel Rochester, the Revolutionary Patriot, whose business enterprise first led to the utilization of the splendid water-power of Western New York.

At the present day, Powers' Commercial Fire-proof Buildings are so identified with the business interests and material progress of the city, that to describe Rochester and make no mention of Powers' Block, would be like presenting the play of Hamlet with the part of Hamlet left out.

In 1812, a rude log cabin was reared upon the present site of this fine structure. This log house was succeeded, in 1818, by the Ensworth House, a wooden frame building, to which, a few years later, there was added an attic, which served as a public hall, and was used successively as a concert-room, ball-room, lecture-room and theatre.

The Ensworth House gave place, under the march of improvement, to the brick edifice which was known for forty years as the Eagle Hotel.

Here, many a political battle was fought, and many a noted guest was entertained. Here, also was reared a gigantic ash pole, in honor of "Harry Clay," in 1844—the lower portion of which was not removed till the excavations were made for the foundations of the present building.

In 1870, Power's building, which is a "city within a city," was completed and thrown open to the public, with its frontage of nearly two hundred feet, upon the principal streets of Rochester—its seven stories of height—its open area in the centre—its grand stair-cases, its superb elevator, its thirty thousand dollars worth of plate glass, its eight acres of flooring, and its *one thousand tenants*, render this building a curiosity and a wonder.

Among the prominent public buildings are the Court House and City Hall, on Buffalo street. The Arcade is also a handsome building. The Western House of Refuge for juvenile offenders is located about one mile from the heart of the city, and was built at a cost of sixty-five thousand dollars.

The Rochester University, Baptist Theological Seminary and Rochester Athenæum, also claim attention.

Among the numerous parks and gardens, the Livingston Place is perhaps the most noticeable. Mount Hope Cemetery, in the vicinity, is a spot of great natural loveliness, and in fact is only considered second in beauty and interest to the famous "Greenwood" of New York.

The cut-stone aqueduct by which the Erie canal is carried across the Genesee river, is worthy of notice.

GENESEE FALLS are seen to the best advantage from the east side of the stream. The railroad cars pass one hundred rods south of the most southerly fall on the Genesee river, so that passengers in crossing, lose the view. To see the Falls to the best advantage, the tourist must cross the bridge over the Genesee, and place himself immediately in front of the fall. This railway bridge is eight hundred feet long, and twenty-five feet high. Some distance beyond, a stairway conducts to the bottom of a ravine, whence you may pass in a boat, or pick your way along beneath the spray of the tumbling floods. The walls of this gorge are of slate stone; they rise to a height of more than three hundred feet, and in the

HUNTING ON LAKE ONTARIO.

many and sudden turnings of the way afford a fine succession of noble pictures.

These Falls have three perpendicular pitches, and two rapids. The first great cataract is eighty rods below the aqueduct, and the ledge here recedes up the river, from the centre to the sides, breaking the water into three distinct sheets. From Table Rock, in the centre of these Falls, Sam Patch made his last, renowned, and fatal leap.

The river below the first fall is broad and deep. Below the second fall, it becomes a rapid, noisy stream, till it reaches the third fall, where it pours its flood over a descent of more than one hundred feet. Below this fall are numerous rapids which continue to Carthage, the head of navigation of the Genesee river from Lake Ontario.

By the Rochester and Charlotte railroad, passengers may reach the shores of Lake Ontario, and thence by steamboats visit almost every port upon the lake—this is a route much traveled by sportsmen, who have learned that hunting in the Lake Ontario region is far from being tame and common-place.

To those who are identified with the cause of "Woman's Rights," Rochester is pleasantly associated with the name of Miss Anthony, although it may surprise the general public, to learn that Rochester is this lady's home when she retires from public into private life.

Ere we say "farewell" to Rochester, we must advert also to the changes which have been wrought in modes of travel within fifty years. Those who step into a railroad car at Albany, at seven o'clock in the morning, and step out to get their dinner in Rochester at two o'clock P. M., will find it difficult to believe that within the memory of by no means the "oldest inhabitant" it required, in muddy seasons of the year, seven nights' and six days' constant traveling in stages to accomplish the same journey.

The rate of progress was not much more swift or agreeable, by the "raging canal." Good stories are told to this day of the exploits by which travelers endeavored to beguile the tedious hours. At one time, among the passengers from Rochester, coming east, were a heavy doctor and sharp lawyer, who were at home, and disposed to be funny during the long and tedious days of canal boat journey by one-horse power.

One day when they were on deck, and the lawyer, who had a hat full of papers on his head, was playing checkers with the captain, the doctor shouted suddenly, "Bridge! low bridge!" The lawyer dropped his head; off went his hat, with all his papers flying into the water. All enjoyed the joke greatly, as the bareheaded lawyer had to jump ashore, and with a boat-hook, fish his documents out of the canal, and then pursue the boat and get aboard as well as he could. He owed the doctor one, and felt bound in law to pay him.

In the afternoon the fat doctor, wearied of sitting, wanted to "stretch his legs" on the tow-path. The boat was steered near the shore; he made a desperate leap, and landed on all fours. But the risk was so great that he said he would walk to Albany rather than attempt to jump aboard. What was to be done? The captain told him to go ahead, and swing down from the next bridge, and he would give the word when to drop. The doctor did as he was told. The boat came under. "Captain," said the lawyer, "let me give the word, and I'll treat the crowd." "Done," said the captain. Slowly the boat moved under the suspended man. "Don't drop till we give the word," cried the captain. Just as the boat cleared him, "Now drop!" shouted the lawyer, and down went the doctor plump into five feet of water.

Like a hippopotamus, the heavy man of medicine waded to the bank; and the boat held up while the lawyer went ashore, gave his hand to the doctor, and pulled him out, whispering, "We're even now!"

Avon lies south of Rochester, some eighteen miles, and is connected with that city by a branch railway—it is also located upon one of the branches of the Erie road. Avon is upon the right bank of the Genesee river, on a terrace one hundred feet above the water, and commands beautiful views in every direction.

There are mineral springs here, and life in summer weather partakes of the gay, social nature which gives to all these summer resorts—"the Springs"—so much of the character of a perpetual pic-nic.

The early mornings are spent in walks and conversation; and at half-meridian the bath-houses swarm with bathers. Then billiards, and croquet, occupy the time till early dinner. Toward evening, riding parties start off in every direction with a hilarity that keeps the more serious invalids in good humor till their return. Thus the days and nights are passed at Avon.

Three Water Cures have recently been opened here! *May they all prosper!* Such institutions seem peculiarly adapted to the summer wants of those who visit mineral springs in search of the magic Fountain of Health. But what dreary winter homes they must be to the invalid, who should be surrounded with cheerful scenes. Probably the prestige of the noted New York Water Cure at Laight street, New York city, is due in part to its location in the Metropolis, as well as to the success of its medical treatment. For the winter, it must be a retreat far preferable to these Cures in Western New York, and at *all* seasons the well known Laight street Water Cure and Hygienic Home proffers its hospitalities to those who visit the city. It is not to be wondered at, that many wealthy and cultured citizens from all parts of the Empire State, make the Hygienic Home their *Hotel*, when in New York.

While at Avon, it should be remarked that we are still in that region which was once the home of the Seneca Indians. In this tribe the poetic sentiment was more highly developed than is usual with "the poor Indian."

A beautiful superstition prevailed among them. When a maiden died, they imprisoned a young bird till it began to try its power of song—then, loading it with messages and caresses, the women of the tribe would loose its bonds over the grave, believing that it would not fold its wings or close its eyes, until, in the spirit land, it had delivered its precious burden of affection to the loved and lost. It was not infrequent for twenty or thirty birds to be set free above one grave.

Upon the banks of the Genesee river, near the village of Geneseo, once stood the famous "Big Tree." When the white man first saw it, it was the patriarch of the Genesee Valley, and was so revered by the Senecas, that they named the beautiful savanna around it, and their village near it, "Big Tree." It also gave name to an eminent Seneca chief, the coadjutor and friend of Cornplanter, Half-town, Farmers-brother, and other great leaders of the warlike Seneca nation.

In the autumn of 1779, Sullivan, with a chastising army, swept so ruthlessly through their beautiful land, annihilating villages, and leaving sombre tracks of desolation behind him, that Washington, "chief of the pale-faces," who was held responsible for the act, was called The Town Destroyer. "When your army entered the Six Nations," said Corn-planter to Washington, in 1792, "we called you 'The Town Destroyer;' and to this day, when that name is heard, our women look behind them and turn pale, and our children cling close to the necks of their mothers."

The age of the Big Tree was doubtless more than a thousand years. Little of it was left at last but its mighty trunk, which measured twenty-six feet in circumference. A vigorous elm germinated beneath its roots, and clasped one of its larger but decayed branches, seeming like another Æneas piously bearing old Anchises in its filial arms. But it was a treacherous friend. It robbed the old tree of its needed sustenance, and hour by hour, while it twined its young branches lovingly among the gnarled ones of the patriarch, it drew from it its life-blood. A local writer happily compared the relationship to the contact of the hardy Indian with the white man, and wrote:

> " Crushed in the Saxon's treacherous grasp,
> The Indian's heart is broke :
> The graceful elm's insidious clasp
> Destroys the mighty oak !"

During a great flood, early in November, 1857, both the Big Tree and the treacherous elm were swept away by the raging waters of the Genesee river.

BUFFALO AND NIAGARA.

XI.

BUFFALO is frequently called the "beautiful city." It is seen in its brightest aspect by travelers who arrive in the early evening, or in the cool of the morning, by trains from the east or west, and, after satisfying wants of the inner man, ride or stroll over the city.

Fine edifices are very plentiful here—the Buffalo University—the State Normal School—the State Insane Asylum—the Female Academy, with an endowment of fifty thousand dollars, etc. Five, fine public squares, and a profusion of shade trees, relieve, and set off, the pleasant looking dwelling-houses.

Here resides Mark Twain—the "inimitable Mark."

Here, also, comes corn, not only from Chicago, but from all the ports around the lakes.

Here, too, may be seen, in its glory, the Elevator, that amphibious institution, which flourishes only on the banks of navigable waters.

An elevator is probably as ugly and as useful a monster as has yet been produced in a country which boasts itself of wondrous contrivances—in patent remedies for the usually troublous operations of life.

Buffalo is a gateway through which *eighty million* bushels of breadstuffs have passed eastward in one year. Let those who are susceptible of statistics, muse on this.

The city gradually rises as it recedes from the water's edge, and at the distance of two miles becomes an extended plain, fifty feet above the level of the harbor, affording delightful views of the city, Niagara Lake and Canada shore.

From Buffalo, five trains run daily to Niagara Falls.

NIAGARA. has been our goal. We have traveled here by devious ways—have seen much water upon our road, and have had to talk of at least a score of water-falls, but feeling that we are not particularly happy in describing water-falls, we have tried to keep what little capacity we do possess, to assist our description of Niagara. And now that we are here, words fail us!

What can we say that has not been often said, and *better said*, before?

Yet of all sights upon our broad earth which people travel to see, Niagara may justly claim to bear away the palm!

In the list of such sights, we intend to include all buildings, pictures, statues—all wonders of art created by man, and all wonders of nature created by God.

Those who have traveled but little, may doubt,—those who have traveled widely, will confirm this view.

Yet this is not saying that Niagara should be seen in preference to all the works of art and nature which we claim that it excels.

At Florence, there may be gained a mastery of modern art; at Rome, an understanding of the cold hearts, correct eyes and cruel ambition of the old Latin race. In Switzerland, the grandeur and loveliness of nature will stir the springs of romance in every human soul. The Tropics will unfold a new world of strange luxuriance and gorgeous effects! At Paris, there has been seen in the past, and will be seen again, the world's varnish—its supreme of polish, shining, superficial and unreal! London and New York reveal *man's power*, the gigantic machinery of trade! But there is no other *one* thing so beautiful, so glorious, and so powerful as Niagara.

Any one of the journeys we have mentioned may—nay, they *must*—be more valuable to a man than a journey to Niagara. At Niagara, there is that fall of waters alone. Yet that fall is more graceful than Giotto's Tower, more noble than the Apollo! The peaks of the Alps are not so astounding in their solitude! The valleys of the Blue Mountains, in Jamaica, are less green. The finished glaze of the Second Empire in Paris was less invaluable. The full tide of trade around the Bank of England, and in "down town," New York, is not so inexorably powerful.

That the waters of Lake Erie have come down in their courses from the broad basins of Lake Michigan, Lake Superior and Lake Huron; that these waters fall into Lake Ontario by the short and rapid river of Niagara, called by the Indians, "Thunder of Waters," and that the Falls of Niagara are made by a sudden break in the level of this rapid river, is undoubtedly known to all who will read these pages.

"Where shall we stop at Niagara?" becomes now a question of more importance, than any consideration of the causes which have produced Niagara?

There are hotels upon the Canadian, and hotels on the American shore. The patriotic, however, who do not belong to that class of whom it said, that good Americans go to Paris when they die—will undoubtedly *spend their money in our own country!* The greater variety of prospect can also be had on the American shore.

The Falls were first seen by a white man—a Jesuit Missionary—in 1678. How many thousands have been here since, it is impossible to determine. A few years ago, life at Niagara was quite burdensome because of the rapacious and every where present hackmen. This class, however, are now quite subdued. They are *chained* into a very limited space at the railroad depot; and when the cars arrive, bringing innocent strangers, all they can do is to hail them gently from their cage, and see if, by chance, any body wants to ride. The arrangement is really very comfortable. And though of course, if you go outside of your hotel, a hackman pops up at every street corner, yet, on the whole, they do not annoy travelers half as much as they used to do.

Directions how to view Niagara are altogether superfluous—the crowd—the guides—and the roar of the great Cataract, being indications which no one will err in following.

The Falls are made, by a sudden breach in the level of the river, but never elsewhere, as far as the world yet knows, has a breach so sudden been made in a river carrying in its channel any such body of water. Above the falls, for more than a mile, the water frets itself into little torrents, and begins to assume the majesty of its power.

The waters, though so broken in their descent, are deliciously green. This color will be better seen from the further end of Iris, or Goat Island, which divides the river immediately above the Falls.

Indeed, Goat Island is a part of that precipitously broken ledge, over which the river tumbles, and will in time doubtless, like Table Rock, crumble away, Let us hope that the time will be very long.

In the meanwhile, Goat Island is perhaps a mile round, and heavily covered with timber. It is connected by a fine bridge with the main shore.

BATH ISLAND is reached by a bridge from Goat Island; and beyond Goat Island there are a few scattered rocks, which are connected with it by a third bridge. These rocks lie on the very brink of the precipice, between the American Falls and the Horse-Shoe Fall, and on them stands the tower, named Terrapin or Prospect Tower, from which we obtain a magnificent view of Niagara, and especially of the Horse-Shoe Fall, where the line of the ledge bends inwards against the flood—in, and in, and in, till one is led to think that the depth of that Horse-Shoe is immeasurable.

It has been cut with no stinting hand. A monstrous cantle has been worn out back of the centre of the rock, so that the fury of the waters converges, and the spectator, as he gazes into the hollow, with wishful eyes, fancies that he can hardly trace out the centre of the abyss.

> "Flow on forever, in thy glorious robe
> Of terror and of beauty. Yea, flow on,
> Unfathomed and resistless. God hath set
> His rainbow on thy forehead, and the cloud
> Mantled around thy feet.
> Thou dost speak
> Alone of God, who poured thee as a drop
> From his right hand."

From Prospect Tower, the view of the Falls is not as entire and complete, as from the Canadian shore, but it is perhaps more beautiful.

The eye in roving over the landscape at this point, cannot fail to perceive on the Canadian side, up above the fall, what Mr. Anthony Trollope, a recent visitor, calls, a "horrid obelisk, put there with some camera obscura intention for which the projector deserves to be put into Coventry."

NIAGARA

"At such a place as Niagara, tasteless buildings, run up in wrong places, with a view of money making, are perhaps necessary evils. It may be that they are not evils at all; that they give more pleasure than pain, seeing that they tend to the enjoyment of the multitude. But there are edifices of this description which cry aloud to the gods, by the force of their own ugliness and malposition. As to such, it may be said that there should somewhere exist a power capable of crushing them in their birth. This obelisk or picture-building at Niagara, is one of such!"

Very creditable photographs of the Falls, and of visitors, are taken there, however, and perhaps the building does not generally incur the maledictions which Mr. Trollope expends upon it.

On Goat Island, is the *Indian Emporium*, an amusing place to visit, but it may be surmised that some members of the "universal Yankee nation" have a hand in the manufacture of the Indian curiosities sold here.

From the Indian emporium, three routes diverge over the island. The principal path is that to the right, which keeps the best of the sights till the last—affording less striking views of the Falls than do the other routes, at first, but surpassing them both at its conclusion.

Taking the right-hand path, then from the Toll Gate, we reach first, the center Fall, called the *Cave of the Winds*, midway between the American and the Horse-Shoe Fall.

The Cave is one hundred feet high, and of the same extent in width. A wonderful prospect may be securely enjoyed here. Magical rainbow pictures may frequently be seen, and the *three profiles* are always objects of interest. These profiles, seemingly some two feet long, are to be seen, one directly above the other, as you look across the first sheet of water, directly under the lowest point of rock.

Luna Island is reached by a foot-bridge, from the right of Goat Island. Those who watch for the rainbow here will understand the fitness of the island's name. Lives have been lost here, and many a tale of disaster or hair-breadth escape is told as we pass along.

Biddle's Stairs are upon the west side of the island, and were named in honor of Nicholas Biddle, of United States Bank fame, who is reported to have said to the workmen: "Make us something, by which we may descend and see what is below." These spiral stairs are secured to the rocks by strong fastenings.

This vicinity is noted for the exploits of Sam Patch, the famous jumper, who averred that "one thing might be done as well as another."

Gull Island is in view, upon which the foot of man has never trod. The Three Sisters are small islands near; and a spot named the Bathing Place of Francis Abbot, the Hermit, who long resided here, is pointed out.

At the head of Goat Island, is Navy Island, where occurred many scenes in the Canadian Rebellion, known as McKensie's War.

Grand Island, which contains eleven thousand acres, is the spot upon which Major M. M. Noah once hoped to assemble all the Hebrew tribes.

From the American shore, a descent of two hundred feet by staircase, brings one to the Ferry which runs to the Canadian shore, three-fourths of a mile distant. It is by this crossing that the best conception is attained of the power and majesty of the tremendous Cataract of Niagara.

In 1869, a fine Suspension Bridge for carriages and pedestrians was completed just below the Falls, connecting the village of Niagara Falls with Clifton, thus obviating the necessity of the long ride around by the old Suspension Bridge into Canada.

THE WHIRLPOOL, three miles below the Falls, corresponds with the famous Maelstrom, on the coast of Norway. A difficult path leads to a point where a full view of it may be obtained.

THE DEVIL'S HOLE, a mile below the Whirlpool, embraces about two acres, cut out laterally and perpendicularly in the rock by the side of the river, and is one hundred and fifty feet deep. Those who are not content with a *carriage* view, but will alight, and walk to the further side of the flat projecting rock, will be richly repaid for their trouble.

CHASM TOWER, three and a half miles below the Falls, commands a suberb prospect of the surrounding country.

TABLE ROCK is no more. Its history is left us. It fell in 1862, but its vicinity is still a famous place of resort, where the Cataract's roar transcends all lesser sounds.

TERMINATION ROCK occupies a recess behind the great Horse-Shoe Fall. It is approached by the descent of a spiral staircase, and the traverse of a narrow and fearful path through the blinding spray *behind the mighty Fall*.

It is an excursion which offers peril and delight to the *real* Tourist. Let not the timid, and ease-loving—the fair weather traveler rashly attempt thus to see Niagara.

THE MUSEUM, near Table Rock, contains more than ten thousand specimens of minerals, birds and animals, many of which were collected in the vicinity of the Falls.

The Burning Spring is two miles above the Falls. Its water emits a brilliant flame when a fee has rewarded the attendant, for its ignition.

The height of the American Fall is one hundred and sixty-four feet, that of the Canadian or Horse-Shoe, one hundred and fifty feet. The former is nine hundred feet across, and the latter one thousand nine hundred.

The roar of the waters has been heard at Toronto, forty-four miles away. It is asserted by some, that Niagara in winter affords the most sublime spectacle of all, but we are among those who prefer to serve Queen June, rather than King Frost!

The Battle Ground of Lundy's Lane, where in 1814, occurred a noted contest between the English and American forces, is about a mile and a half distant from the Clifton House. Lewiston and Queenston, about seven miles distant from the Falls, are also worthy of a visit.

Of Niagara, it is related, that at one hotel, one summer Sabbath day last season, seventy-five Brides sat down to dine at the table " d'Hote."

Church's Niagara, one of the famous pictures of the times, has, we learn, recently passed into the possession of Mr. A. T. Stewart.

But every one who travels, visits Niagara! Its story is an oft-told tale. With the crowds we came hither—we stay a day, or a week—and then gayly say, " *Niagara, Farewell!*"

[This Engraving is incorrect in the Piazzas on the wings, which are not built; and in omitting numerous large trees in front.]

COOPER HOUSE,
Otsego Lake, Cooperstown, N. Y.

The Cooper House stands eighty feet above the Lake; 1,200 feet above the Sea; in a fine Park of over seven acres, handsomely embellished, planted with Shade Trees, and including Croquet, Ball and Archery Grounds. All modern improvements, including bells, gas in every room, hot and cold baths, &c. The house accommodates **300 GUESTS**, and is well adapted for families.

On the enlarged premises have been erected **Summer Houses, Bowling Alleys and Billiard Room**, a new Laundry, Barns with increased stabling accommodations, etc.

A **NEW STEAMER** on Otsego Lake, accommodating 30 persons, will run regularly in connection with the Railroad, and **RICHFIELD** and **SHARON SPRINGS**, besides making frequent **Pleasure Trips** around the Lake, which is also supplied with numerous sail and row boats. Omnibusses will run regularly from the Cooper House, to and from the Steamer and favorite prospects, etc.

Cooperstown is within about four hours from **ALBANY** or **BINGHAMTON** by rail, and from **UTICA** by rail, stage, and Otsego Lake Steamer, twice each way daily; of easy access from, and in telegraphic communication with all parts of the world. Albany morning papers are received at noon, and New York dailies the same evening. Richfield and Sharon Springs are a delightful drive and sail of two or three hours.

To those seeking health, who enjoy nature's beauties in hill, lake, and valley scenery, who are fond of walks and drives, picturesque and charming in variety and extent, and of boating on one of the most beautiful inland lakes in the State, Cooperstown offers rare inducements, while the historic and classic associations of Cooper's pen give to the region a special prominence.

Board, $4 per day, or from $18 to $25 per week; for one month or over, at the rate of $15 to $20 per week, according to size and location of room. Families accommodated after August on very favorable terms.

COLEMAN & MAXWELL.

WM. B. COLEMAN,   ALBERT MAXWELL,
Of the New York Hotel.   Late Supt. of the Union Club.

Many Changes have been wrought within Fifty Years.

Steamboats, Railways, Inventions and Improvements have followed each other in close succession, yet that which is of real value outlives the march of change, and permanency is often a genuine test of merit.

The Lucius Hart Manufacturing Company,

Whose place of business is represented above, have been for FORTY YEARS established at the same well-known stand, 4 and 6 BURLING SLIP, at the foot of John Street, New York City. Britannia Ware was the fashionable metal, ranking next to Solid Silver, forty years ago, and MR. HART, the Senior Member of the Firm, won a splendid reputation as an HONEST MANUFACTURER of it. The experience of every purchaser proved that all goods stamped with the name of LUCIUS HART were of Sterling Value. Twenty-three years since, when Electro Plating became popular, the manufacture of Silver Plated Ware was added to that of Britannia by the Lucius Hart Company.

This is the Oldest Firm in the United States engaged in the Business of making Silver Plated Ware.

In buying plated ware, it is especially important to deal with men of reputation and integrity, for the buyer has no means of testing the thickness of the silver plating until time and use conclusively test it for him. The goods made by the Lucius Hart Manufacturing Co. are widely known as possessing substantial value. Their business is immense—in the article of Ice Pitchers alone their sales far exceed ALL the sales of two or three of their most prominent competitors in this line of trade. They have now about thirty new and elegant patterns of Ice Pitchers for sale at the most Reasonable Prices. COMMUNION SERVICES are also a specialty in their manufacture. Persons residing in any part of the State will in most cases save the expense of their trip by visiting New York, and making their purchases of Ice Pitchers and other plated ware of the Lucius Hart Co. Their place of business is easily found, at

4 & 6 BURLING SLIP,
Foot of John Street, New York City.

HINTS FOR TRAVELERS.

XII.

THIS is the era of Summer trips and Honeymoon tours—of travel, domestic and foreign invasion. This is the epoch when anywhere on the road, say, from New York to Niagara, you encounter now and again a young lady in a suit of brown or gray, matched from gloves to gaiters, not loquacious, but blissful, protected by a young gentleman who perpetually pulls the car-blinds up and down, arranges shawls, runs for glasses of water, and does not read the paper.

For these travelers, few hints are needful. They stop only at the grand hotels—they journey only on the broad thoroughfares which lead to fashionable resorts, where the bridal trousseau will be properly appreciated.

There is a larger class who journey for genuine pleasure, anywhere that the mood of the moment, or the recommendation of friends, or the descriptions of the Guide Books may lead them.

To the consideration of these travelers, we present a few timely and (homely) suggestions.

A waterproof cloak is the best umbrella. Unless you are fond of "spread eagles," do not wear a shawl upon a windy summit. Ladies who wish while traveling to have a suit made in haste, will find at 670 Broadway, Albany, one of the best Dress-making establishments in the State.

At Saratoga, it is said that if you rub the outside rim of the ear with a little cologne, or spirits of ammonia, you will keep delightfully cool on the hottest day. This recipe is easily tried.

The mosquito, as a public singer, draws well, but never gives satisfaction, whereupon the Rev. Henry Ward Beecher declares that tobacco has its uses, as well as its abuses, and that it is one of the best remedies for stings of insects. "Wet it so that the juice shall start, put it on the place stung, and in one moment you are all right."

To prevent *Mosquitoes or Gnats* from annoying you,—mix sweet oil and tar in equal parts. All manner of insects abhor the smell of tar. When therefore you fish, or hunt, or journey, where they may be expected, pour a little into the palm of your hand, and anoint your face with it. To most persons, the scent of tar is not offensive, and the mixture washes off on the first application of soap and water, leaving no trace or taint. To reconcile the ladies to it, we add the fact that it renders the skin soft and smooth as an infant's. If a different protection is preferred, a mask may be made from a yard and a half of fine Swiss mull, gathered with an elastic band in the form of a sack or bag. Have the elastic so as to slip over the head, which, when you have done, fix the elastic inside the collar-band, and you can laugh defiance at mosquitoes and other torments, but whether you can breathe very comfortably is doubtful. This device is frequently resorted to in the Adirondacks, but in our opinion is neither as agreeable or convenient as the dose of tar and oil.

The hands should be protected by a pair of common buckskin gloves, to which an armlet of chamois should be fitted which will reach to the elbow, and there button tightly around, leaving no opening, however small, at the wrists, by which the gnats may creep up the arm.

The traveler who meets with "the vexing flea," will find a piece of soft and fine flannel, if he will lie down on it at night, will be preferred by his fleaship, who likes the softest and the warmest couch. When the flea has taken up his camp for the night, upon the flannel, by a little adroitness on your part, his career may be speedily brought to an end.

The best cure for Sea sickness is to administer as much cayenne pepper as the patient can possibly bear, in a bowl of hot broth or soup. All nausea will soon disappear.

A simple, safe and certain cure for the *colds in the head*, which are apt to annoy travelers, will be found in simple Tincture of Iodine. Ladies especially are liable to bring away "a sneeze, a wheeze and a sniffle," as one of their credentials, showing that they have been "in the country," and Iodine is particularly recommended for their benefit. Hold the vial containing it for some time in the hand, and on unstopping, it will be found that the warmth of the hand causes the evaporation of the Iodine, which must be faithfully inhaled several times—and the inhalations repeated once in three minutes, until every symptom of the cold has passed off. The bottle must be supplied with a glass stopper, as Iodine will consume a cork.

This remedy is prescribed by a very celebrated physician, as one which is attended with no ill effects.

In respect to the selection of boarding places for the summer, if you have little ones to accompany, *do* consult their interests.

JACKSON MILITARY INSTITUTE

(ESTABLISHED IN 1857,)

TARRYTOWN-ON-THE-HUDSON.

Location Healthy; Buildings and Grounds ample and attractive, Instruction thorough. Education, in its true and proper sense, being the just development of ALL OUR POWERS, Physical, Mental, Moral and Social. The policy of the School is to send forth in the person of each Pupil a sound mind in a sound body, regulated by sound morality; producing, in all respects, the pattern of full-grown Men. Inspection invited. Send for Circular.

REV. F. J. JACKSON, M. A., Principal and Proprietor.

SMITHSONIAN HOUSE,
NYACK-ON-THE-HUDSON.

OPEN JUNE 1ST, AS A STRICTLY FIRST-CLASS BOARDING HOUSE.

City Comforts, most Healthful Location, Large, Airy, Well-Furnished Rooms, Gas, Pure Water, Shaded Grounds, Magnificent Views, Boating and Riding easily attainable, Good Table.

Transient as well as Permanent Boarders will be made welcome.

PRICES REASONABLE.

Address M. L. BIGELOW, Nyack-on-the-Hudson.

NORTH RIVER & NEW YORK
STEAMBOAT COMPANY.
NEW YORK OFFICE
On Harrison St. Pier.

The above Line of Boats run Daily (Sundays excepted,)

Between Peekskill and New York,

Touching at all intermediate Landings.

Leaving New York, foot of Harrison Street,

Every Afternoon at 3½, 4 and 4½ o'clock,

Returning to the City about 10 A. M.

FREIGHT CARRIED BY THIS LINE
ON THE MOST REASONABLE TERMS.

1871.   **E. LANE, Agent.**

Those city mothers who have growing children with pale faces, slender forms, and delicate appetites, will reap their reward next fall if they will discard fashion, and take their little ones where they can have simple food, plenty of exercise and fresh air, and where it is sufficient to dress them only *neatly*. A week or two at a stylish watering place, as a change or amusement, may not be harmful; but the necessity imposed upon mothers at so many of these resorts to dress children in the highest style, is ruinous to the little folks, and an anxious care for the mother. Do not let the children grow up prematurely into men and women. Keep them fresh, simple and natural as long as possible.

As bathing is one of the most popular of summer amusements, and one which is often attended with ill consequences, we copy the directions which have been recently issued to bathers by the Royal Humane Society of London. They are worthy of consideration:

"Avoid bathing within two hours after a meal.

"Avoid bathing when exhausted from any cause.

"Avoid bathing when the body is cooling after perspiration; but bathe when the body is warm, provided no time is lost in getting into the water.

"Avoid remaining too long in the water; leave the water immediately when there is the slightest feeling of chilliness.

"Avoid bathing altogether in the open air, if after having been a short time in the water, there is a sense of chilliness with numbness of the hands and feet.

"The vigorous and strong may bathe early in the morning on an emp'y stomach.

"The young and those that are weak had better bathe three hours after a meal; the best time for such is from two to three hours after breakfast.

"Those who are subject to attacks of giddiness and faintness, and those who suffer from diseases of the heart, should not bathe without first consulting their medical adviser."

THE DONALD-HIGHLAND INSTITUTE,

HIGHLAND FALLS, N. Y.

A SELECT BOARDING SCHOOL FOR BOYS,

Occupying the "OAK GROVE COTTAGE" PREMISES, within two miles of WEST POINT MILITARY ACADEMY, and near COZZENS' HOTEL.

THIRD YEAR OPENS SEPTEMBER 21st, 1871.

SPECIAL ADVANTAGES IN FITTING FOR WEST POINT.

References and Information concerning its Location, Appointments, Charges and Work, will be given to Parents on applying personally, or by letter to

ROBERT DONALD, A. M., Principal.

CLARENDON HOUSE,

NYACK-ON-THE-HUDSON.

MRS. H. B. ADAMS,

Long and favorably known in St. Paul, Minnesota, has opened the CLARENDON for the Accommodation of Guests.

The House is beautifully situated; Rooms well-arranged and airy, commanding Fine Views of the River.

NOTICE TO THE LADIES.

Among the many useful Inventions produced by the Nineteenth Century, none occupies a more prominent position than that of the Sewing Machine. The cheerful hum of these tireless little helpmates of our mothers and wives may now be heard in almost every house in the land. They are made in endless variety, and one is almost at a loss to choose when there are so many of decided merit. One of the latest and most improved is the **EMPIRE**, manufactured by the **Empire Sewing Machine Co., 294 Bowery, N. Y.;** SPEEDY, NOISELESS and DURABLE; and we can conscientiously recommend parties in search of a Machine to give it an examination before concluding to purchase.

Agents wanted, liberal discounts given.

PRINCESS NEMONA;

OR, LOVE IN THE EMPIRE STATE.

XIII.

NOT a day's ride from Port Kent, and not far distant from the road that leads to North Elba, the Au Sable river takes a short leap called the Maiden's Falls.

There are two love stories linked with the Maiden's Falls, one of which is told freely, while the other is whispered pitifully among the few who know the young girl to whom it relates.

A hundred years ago, or thereabouts, the Princess Nemona was the belle and beauty of that Indian tribe whose home was usually in this vicinity. A soldier from Quebec, while on an exploring tour, met the red-lipped, graceful Indian girl, and regarded her with an admiration which soon ripened into love.

He offered marriage, but wished, ere the nuptial knot was tied, to obtain the consent of his parents to their union. He proposed to visit Quebec to consult them, and then to come for his bride,

FREEMAN & BURR,

138 & 140 Fulton St., N. Y.

FREEMAN & BURR have very great pleasure in inviting an inspection of their immense Stock for the present season. The choicest products of the Loom, from all parts of the world, have been laid under contribution in making selections, which will be found, both in the piece and made up for immediate wear, for all ages and all occasions.

SUITS, $10.	COATS, $5.	PANTS, $3.	VESTS, $2.	BOYS'	SUITS, $5.
SUITS, $15.	COATS, $8.	PANTS, $4.	VESTS, $3.	BOYS'	SUITS, $8.
SUITS, $20.	COATS, $10.	PANTS, $6.	VESTS, $4.	BOYS'	SUITS, $10.
SUITS, $30.	COATS, $18.	PANTS, $8.	VESTS, $5.	BOYS'	SUITS, $12.
SUITS, $40.	COATS, $24.	PANTS, $10.	VESTS, $6.	BOYS'	SUITS, $15.
SUITS, $50.	COATS, $30.	PANTS, $12.	VESTS, $8.	BOYS'	SUITS, $20.

ORDERS BY LETTER PROMPTLY FILLED.

Freeman & Burr's Easy and Accurate System for SELF-MEASURE enables parties in any part of the country to order clothing direct from them, with the certainty of receiving the most PERFECT FIT attainable.

Rules for Self-Measure, Samples of Goods, Price List, and Fashion Sheet, sent Free on application.

BLEES'

Noiseless Link Motion, Lock Stitch Shuttle

Family Sewing Machine,

WILL

HEM, BRAID, GATHER, TUCK, RUFFLE, CORD, BIND, FRILL, QUILT, FRINGE, FELL, &c,

Challenges the World in Perfection of Work, Strength and Beauty of Stitch, Durability of Construction, and Rapidity of Motion.

Call and Examine! Send for Circulars!

AGENTS WANTED.

Manufactured by

BLEES' SEWING MACHINE CO.,
623 Broadway, New York.

who had pledged herself to renounce her forest life, and accompany him to the home of the pale-face.

They parted by the Falls, and she vowed to sit at nightfall at their tryst, during his absence, to dream of him, and await his return.

But he came not.

A year rolled slowly and heavily away. Nemona mourned for him silently, as it befitted a Chief's daughter to mourn a faithless lover.

Tidings came at last, that he had been slain by hostile Indians on his returning way. Then Nemona smiled! His death was preferable to his desertion! She clad herself in royal robes, and watched the sun set at their tryst, chanting a dirge for the "Brave who was slain in the summer time."

When twilight threw its mantle over the earth—with the death-wail still upon her lips—the maiden sprang lightly over the Falls, and went to meet her lover on the "Happy Hunting Grounds," while her story is told at the "Maiden's Fall," to this very day!

A little, lonely hamlet is near these falls. Some forty scattered houses constitute the entire settlement. Many of the inhabitants are charcoal burners. A few are farmers who till the sterile soil.

To this spot, so nearly out of the world, thirty years ago came a man who was stricken with sorrow more than with years, bringing with him a motherless babe. He was a recluse and misanthrope. Some said that losses of friends and property had unsettled his reason in a measure.

Be that as it may, he built a small house, and imported costly furniture to fill it. He had a trusty Scotch housekeeper, and his child was consigned to her for care and training.

THE NATIONAL
Life Insurance Company of New York,

No. 212 BROADWAY,

Issues all the new forms of Policies, and presents 'as favorable terms as any Company in the United States.

Thirty days' grace allowed on each payment after the first year, and the policy held good during that time.

Dividends declared annually, and available in payment of Premium, reduction of Loans, or increase of amount of insurance.

All of our Policies are INCONTESTIBLE after five annual payments.

Policy-Holders share in the Profits of the Company, and have a voice in the election and management of the Company.

All Policies, when the Premium has been paid in cash, have a CASH SURRENDER VALUE, after three or more annual payments, and after five or more annual payments **an Annuity Bond will be granted** in lieu of the same for as many years as there have been annual cash premiums paid.

No Policy or Medical Fee charged.

All Policies Non-Forfeitable, on the principle of the Massachusetts Law.

EDWARD A. JONES, President.

J. O. HALSEY, Vice-President.   J. A. MORTIMORE, Secretary.

CHAS. G. PEARSON, Assistant Secretary.

CALL OR SEND FOR CIRCULAR.

AGENTS WANTED.

Adele S. blossomed into girlhood as fair and sweet a human flower as ever grew into beauty in the wilderness. Of French descent, she had inherited that bewitching grace from a long line of courtly ancestors which would have rendered her charming, even without the large hazel eyes, *darker than her golden hair*, which lent such lustre to her beauty.

She was but thirteen—a child in years, and a woman at heart—when a stranger visited her home. He came with velvet coat, with rod and gun, a forerunner of that tide of sportsmen, which summer now brings to the Adirondack region, every year. This man was three or four and twenty years of age, handsome and accomplished.

He became the friend and lover of Adele S. Her father was a recluse, and knew nothing of the acquaintance. There was no one, therefore, to interpose. The simple-minded housekeeper, and still more simple villagers, noted the intimacy with secret pride in Adele and her lover, and no questions were asked on her behalf.

Their trysting-place was the Maiden's Fall, and there they parted one August evening.

He returned to his city home, and Adele pined visibly after his departure. In less than a month, fever laid its fervid hand upon the child.

Time passed slowly, and hope went out with the sunlight of an October day. The father stood by her bedside, and the child knew that she was dying. Her last request was, that Arnold —— might be summoned to attend her funeral, for, said she, " he is my lover, and promised to come next year and marry me."

Her request was heeded, and the handsome stranger arrived in time to walk with her father as chief mourner in her funeral train.

BEAUTIFUL WOMEN.

All women know that it is beauty, rather than genius, which all generations of men have worshipped in the sex. Can it be wondered at, then, that so much of woman's time and attention should be directed to the means of developing and preserving that beauty! Women know, too, that when men speak of the intellect of women, they speak critically, tamely, coolly; but when they come to speak of the charms of a beautiful woman, their language and their eyes kindle with enthusiasm which shows them to be profoundly, if not, indeed, ridiculously in earnest. It is part of the natural sagacity of women to perceive all this, and therefore employ every allowable art to become the goddess of that adoration. Preach to the contrary as we may, against the arts employed by women for enhancing their beauty, there still stands the eternal fact, that the world does not prefer the society of an ugly woman of genius to that of a beauty of less intellectual acquirements. The world has yet allowed no higher mission to woman than to be beautiful, and it would seem that the ladies of the present age are carrying this idea of the world to greater extremes than ever, for all women now to whom nature has denied the talismanic power of beauty supply the deficiency by the use of a most delightful toilet article, known as the "Bloom of Youth," which has been lately introduced into this country by GEORGE W. LAIRD, a delicate beautifier, which smoothes out all indentations, furrows, scars, removing tan, freckles, and discolorations from the skin, leaving the complexion clear, brilliant, and beautiful, the skin soft and smooth. With the assistance of this American invention of a Lady's toilet, female beauty is destined to play a larger part in the admiration of men and the ambition of woman than all the arts employed since her creation. This most delightful and harmless Toilet preparation has been established over ten years; during that time over one million ladies have used it, and in every instance given entire satisfaction. Ladies need have no fear of using this invaluable Toilet acquisition.

One of the most eminent Physicians of New York city,

DR. LOUIS A. SAYRE,

After carefully examining the analysis prepared by the CHEMIST OF THE METROPOLITAN BOARD OF HEALTH, of the genuine Laird's "BLOOM OF YOUTH," pronounced the preparation harmless, and entirely free from any ingredient injurious to health.

Ladies, beware of Dangerous and Worthless Imitations of George W. Laird's "Bloom of Youth."

The unprecedented success of George W. Laird's "Bloom of Youth" has influenced unprincipled persons to counterfeit and imitate the "Bloom of Youth." The genuine preparation has achieved great popularity during the last ten years it has been in use.

Mr. Laird, being determined to rid the market of counterfeits, and in order to protect the public from imposition, and to prevent their purchasing not only a worthless but a dangerous imitation of his reliable and Harmless beautifier of the skin, has placed the label of this preparation under the charge of the United States Government, and their Engraver, Mr. Joseph R. Carpenter, of Philadelphia, has prepared a design, and engraved the same on steel plates, at a large expense. The new label will embrace the United States Revenue stamp. Any person or persons counterfeiting this label will be liable to imprisonment by the United States authorities. Beware of worthless imitations. See that the Revenue Stamp is printed on the front label, and the name G. W. Laird is stamped in glass on the back of each bottle. NO OTHER IS GENUINE. This delightful preparation is

Sold by all Druggists and Fancy Goods Dealers.

DEPOT, 5 GOLD ST., NEW YORK.

The excitement and sympathy of the village people was intense. He remained among them, petted and pitied and wept over. The fever then attacked the father of Adele, and Arnold was his attendant till the old man bequeathed to him his slender property, *and died.*

When the new heir had entered into possession, he went away. The house of the dead man was sold in the following spring. It brought but a small sum. His income had been derived from money invested in English stocks. The very day on which the last payment made upon this house was remitted, a party of sportsmen arrived from B., the home of Arnold. When this became known, another fact was straightway developed—*that Arnold, in the interim between his leaving Adele in the previous August, and his return to attend her funeral in October, had married a lady to whom he had been long bethrothed.*

Whether he had played his part in this comic-tragedy in the first place simply from pure love of acting, and afterward tarried from hope of gain, or whether some darker reasons influenced his course, will never be known.

There are those who believe that he poisoned the man whose money he inherited! There are those who would tar and feather the handsome gentleman even at this late day, if he ventured to return to the scene of his early exploits! But he lives and thrives, a prominent lawyer in the City of Brotherly Love.

We heard this story last summer, by the Maiden's Fall, and not far from a simple slab, lettered—

"ADELE,
"Aged Thirteen Years.
" Erected by Her Mourning Lover."

Who wrote the inscription, we know not; Arnold's money paid for it—*so they say!*

ROCKLAND FEMALE INSTITUTE

NYACK,

ON THE HUDSON, N. Y.

This is an Incorporated Academic and Collegiate Seminary for the Education of Young Ladies, under the supervision of the Regents of the University of this State.

It is complete in all its appointments, full of healthy life and vigor in all its departments, and keeps pace with the progressive spirit and the wants of the age.

It has a regular graduating course of Study, embracing the branches usually deemed essential to a substantial and finished Education.

Especial attention is also given to the Fine Arts and to the polite accomplishments which fit woman to adorn society and the home circle.

The departments of Music, Painting and the Modern Languages are well sustained and eminently successful.

Much attention is given to the cultivation of refined manners and to the moral bearing of the Young Ladies of the Institute.

The Fall Term of 1871 will commence September 20th.

For a Catalogue with full particulars, address

Rev. L. DELOS MANSFIELD, A. M.,

President.

CLIMBING UP THE MOUNTAIN;

A Parody of Saxe's Rhyme of the Rail.

BY S. S. COLT.

XIV.

SCRAMBLING thro' the forest,
   Tumbling over ridges,
Driving under fir boughs,
   Tilting on log bridges—
Wheezing up the hill-side,
   Drinking at the fountain—
Bless me, this is pleasant,
   Climbing up the mountain!

Men of different "standing"
   In the eye of Fame,
Are tugging thro' the "debris"
   Pretty much the same;

Smart and clumsy people,
  Birds of every feather,
On the mountain hillocks,
  Tumble round together.

Gentleman from Ireland
  Calls the mountains tall—
Gentleman from H'England
  Thinks them rather small—
Gentleman from Gotham,
  With a Wall street mein,
Thinks these "rocks" the biggest
  He has ever seen!

Gentleman quite old
  Asks, "How far to the summit?"
Lady young and handsome
  Has sadly smashed her bunnit;
Gentleman fat and heavy,
  Sober as a vicar,
Bumps around as dreadfully
  As if he'd been in liquor.

Stranger on the right
  Looking very sunny,
Is obviously telling
  The ladies something funny.
Let us turn inquisitor,
  For the smiles are growing "wide;"
'Faith, the man is quoting
  From COLT'S, TOURIST'S GUIDE.

Ancient single lady
  Very dubiously says,
She would not like *alone*
  To traverse rugged ways;
Roguish looking fellow
  Mutters to the stranger—
She ought to be accustomed
  To *such* a kind of danger!

One thoughtful soul is careful
  Of the luncheon casket—
Knowing we'll be hungry,
  Tightly holds the basket;
Feeling that a smash,
  If it came, would surely
Make an end of all things
  Rather prematurely!

Scrambling thro' the forest,
  Tumbling over ridges,
Driving under fir boughs,
  Tilting on log bridges—
Wheezing up the hill-side,
  Drinking at the fountain—
Bless me, this is pleasant,
  Climbing up the mountain!

ARE YOU GOING TO NEW YORK?

If so, and you wish to stop where you can FEEL AT HOME, and get GOOD FOOD HEALTHFULLY PREPARED, and PLENTY OF IT,

GO TO THE HYGIENIC INSTITUTE,

Nos. 13 and 15 Laight Street.

Horse Cars pass near the door to all parts of the city, making it a very convenient stopping place for persons visiting New York, either upon business or pleasure. Open at all hours, day and night. Board by the day or week, at reasonable rates. Rooms can be secured in advance by writing. Address

WOOD & HOLBROOK, Proprietors,

Nos. 13 & 15 Laight Street, New York.

HERALD OF HEALTH,

$2.00 a year; 20 cents a number; 3 months on trial 25 cents.

Every subscriber for one year who sends $2.00 will be entitled to a PREMIUM BOOK, entitled

HINTS TOWARD PHYSICAL PERFECTION,

Or the Philosophy of Human Beauty,

BY D. H. JACQUES.

Showing how to acquire and retain Bodily Symmetry, Health, and Vigor, and to avoid the infirmities and deformities of Age. It contains 300 pages, and nearly 100 fine Engravings The price of the book is $1 50, yet we propose to give it FREE to each subscriber who sends us $2 00. Address

WOOD & HOLBROOK,

15 Laight St., New York.

A REMARKABLE RECORD.

THE CONNECTICUT MUTUAL LIFE
INSURANCE COMPANY.

[*From "The Spectator" for April.*]

A leading Life Company has entitled itself to the gratitude of all who take any interest in life insurance, by the issue of a condensed statement which covers the transactions of the company for twenty-five years. The figures given in this statement are really an epitome of the life business in this country from the outset to the present time. They represent the operations of a company whose whole history has been a record of honorable dealing and remarkable prosperity.

The statement referred to gives the total receipts and disbursements of the company for twenty-five years, ending December 31, 1870, and is as follows:

Total premiums received	$49,676,293
Paid losses and returned to policy holders	23,445,375
	26,230,918
Required for re-insurance, Dec 1870	21,859,940
Balance of premium receipts	4,370,978
Add interest received and accrued	10,352,702
	14,723,680
Deduct taxes of twenty-five years	715,206
	14,008,474
Twenty-five years' management expenses	5,560,750
Surplus, December 31, 1870	$8,447,724
Liabilities, $652,779.	

Of nearly $50,000,000 paid in by policy-holders, we find that 22.78 per cent was repaid in the form of death claims and, by a curious coincidence, another 22.78 per cent returned to them as the amount of their payments in excess of the cost of insurance. So that the policyholders are shown to have really received back nearly half the amount they paid in and their insurance besides. There seems to be small room for complaint here; and, as we happen to know, the insured rather incline to contemplate their connection with the company with considerable complacency.

When we inquire further, we find that, of what remained of the premium receipts, nearly $22,000,000 is still required, (and reserved most sacredly,) as the re-insurance valuation of unexpired policies; and yet there are $4,000,000 left. The interest received and accrued upon investments during the twenty-five years, (over $10,000,000,) has sufficed to pay 60 per cent of all the losses and expenses consequent upon operations extended through a quarter of a century. And, after all these years a surplus is reported of $8,000,000, which may either be divided among the members or retained for their security against whatever contingency the future may have in store.

The practical results of the life insurance scheme, as here exemplified, prove that the business is not essentially, nor necessarily, one of mystery, contingency, or extravagance. We have shown that the insured themselves have received back, already, 45.56 per cent of the premiums they paid, while a divisible surplus of 16 per cent upon these premiums still remains. The business has been transacted at a ratio of expense which is exceptionally low, we admit, but which only shows what judicious and economical management can accomplish. The expenses of management bear a ratio of 11 per cent to premiums, and only 9.35 to total receipts. The commissions paid for the procurement of $50,000,000 of premiums average only 9.02 per cent. The average rate of interest realized on investments [exclusive of premium notes] is stated to be 8.21 per cent.

We welcome this full record, therefore, as a sufficient reply to all the attacks made upon life insurance, and as pointing out the path which every honest life manager should deem it a privilege to tread.

PECK & HILLMAN, General Agents, State of N. Y.,
STATE STREET, TROY, AND 442 BROADWAY, ALBANY.

SPECIALTIES IN NEWSPAPERS.

IT IS often said that it is not possible for a comic paper to live and flourish in America, because all the papers deal more or less in humor, and carry spice and fun through their columns, or at least have a funny department, wherein they gather much matter of that nature, so that a journal devoted to comicality is apt to be palling to the taste, and soon voted a bore.

It is rather an encouraging sign of the interest our reading public take in matters of morals and religion, that nearly all the secular papers are, in these days, paying special attention to such things, and, particularly on Saturdays and Mondays, make a point of furnishing some religious reading to their patrons. However, this is not likely to run the religious weeklies out of their sphere; because, in the first place, the dailies don't do enough of it to replace those specially devoted to it, and then, too, a large part of the matter consists of citations from the religious papers themselves, or discussions of articles from their columns.

The public interest in religious journalism seems to be at its height. There are many representing the various religious denominations and churches, and some few calling themselves "unsectarian," and laboring to bring about rather a unison of christian sentiment among all the sects. Of these, one of the most notable is the one edited by Rev. Henry Ward Beecher— THE CHRISTIAN UNION. Indeed, nothing that this strong man takes hold of seems to fail to secure at once a large share of public attention and favor. The fastidious, critical NATION says that it is "the ablest, and and destined to become the most popular of American religious journals." It has been in existence not yet two years, but its circulation has attained an extraordinary figure, quite overleaping dozens of the long established papers, and, it is said, larger than any other religious journal in the country with one exception. In addition to the admirable religious spirit of its columns, the careful literary tone, the very interesting general articles and the capital selected miscellany, this paper has had a motive power in its publishers, who offer to their subscribers some very attractive things. This last year they bought the renowned steel-plate known as "Marshall's Household Engraving of Washington," and GIVING AWAY a fine impression of it to each subscriber to the paper, ($3 being the yearly subscription price,) have had to send out over 20,000 of these fine engravings in less than eight months! For the next year they offer the Washington still to those who want it, but their main attraction, outside of their excellent paper, is the pair of Chromos known as "Wide Awake" and "Fast Asleep"—of which thousands have been sold at $10 in the picture stores. These pretty English Chromos cannot be bought any cheaper now, but they can be had FOR NOTHING by subscribing to THE CHRISTIAN UNION for one year. The address of the publishers is J. B. Ford & Co., 27 Park Place, New York. They attend to all subscriptions sent them, and give employment to canvassing agents, hundreds of whom made handsome pay last year canvassing for the paper and the picture. We predict another "rush of subscribers" for the coming year.

FINIS.

XV.

THUS our journey Through the Empire State draweth to a close. We have pursued no beaten path—have wandered to and fro, as happy summer Tourists do, passing commendation or criticism upon the places we have visited, as our own experience and judgment have justified our doing.

To that which has been told before concerning the places we have seen, we have added information and items relating to the Past, Present and Future, according as the guardian angel of the "chiel whae has been takin' notes" has cast such favors in our way.

In compiling the TOURIST'S GUIDE, we have traversed the length and the breadth of our noble State, and have nearly everywhere found charming scenery, and refined and hospitable society —fair towns and cities from which we were loth to depart. Good people of this great-hearted State, it has been *our* experience that ye more gladly "welcome the coming," than ye "speed the parting guest!"

THE TOURIST'S GUIDE. 221

For aid in writing and illustrating the TOURIST'S GUIDE, we desire most gratefully to acknowledge our indebtedness to the kindness and courtesy of Mr. H. F. Phinney, of Cooperstown, N. Y., whose interest in every effort, however humble, which tends to gather in a popular form such recollections of the past, and records of the present, as New York State people will not " willingly let die," has led him to place at our disposal much that is of interest, which would have otherwise been to us, in a great measure, unattainable.

Our best thanks are due to this gentleman for the use of the fine engravings of Cooperstown, and Leatherstocking's Falls, which adorn our pages.

To the great Publishing Firm of Messrs. Harper Brothers, of New York, our acknowledgments are due, for the views of the residence of Fenimore Cooper, and of his grave—these superb and costly engravings having been recently procured, at great expense, for their own publications.

The genial kindness of Professor Eastman, of Poughkeepsie—the courtesies of Mr. W. Jennings Demorest, of New York, the popular publisher of " Demorest's Magazine," and " Young America "—and of Mr. S. R. Wells, of New York, with the valuable assistance of Messrs. J. B. Ford & Co., also claim our grateful recognition.

The views of Manhattan Island, in 1609, Neiuw Amsterdam in 1650, Minuit's Purchase of the Island of Manhattan, which is a copy of the large painting now in the possession of the New York Historical Society—and Washington's Head Quarters at Newburgh, are taken by permission of Messrs. Ford & Co., the publishers, from Hon. S. S. Randall's " History of the State of New York," which is the only attempt to condense within small and compact limits, the story of our great State. Mr. Randall, who has been for years the Superintendent of Public Instruction in New York city, has done a work which needed to be done, and done it well, in presenting this book to the people and to the use of our schools.

From other sources, too, we have received aid and encouragement, in our labor of writing of the Empire State, which is now ended here, with a pleasant, " Fare you well," to readers and friends.

LIGHT AND PROFITABLE WORK
Three Popular Publications for Canvassing.
"A LIBRARY OF POETRY AND SONG,"
A choice compilation of 500 volumes in one. 800 pages, 8vo., illustrated. Edited by WILLIAM CULLEN BRYANT.

THE LIFE OF JESUS, THE CHRIST,
BY HENRY WARD BEECHER.
About 450 pages, 8 vo, illustrated. A great work by a great man.

THE CHRISTIAN UNION,
A Weekly Family Journal. "The most able and popular of American Religious Periodicals. Editor, HENRY WARD BEECHER.
To every Subscriber is *given away*, either Marshall's Steel Engraving of "*Washington*," (price $5,) or a *pair* of English Chroms, (price $10.) *Subscription price $3 00 per year.* Agents may address for circulars and terms,
J. B. FORD & CO., 27 Park Place, New York.

A GREAT OFFER!
Only $3 for $11 in Value.
The beautiful and artistic Chromo, "ISN'T SHE PRETTY."
Size, 13 x 17 after Lillie M. Spencer, retail price, $8 00; sent by mail securely done up, post free, as a premium to every yearly subscriber to

DEMOREST'S ILLUSTRATED MONTHLY,
acknowledged the most practical, useful, original Parlor Magazine.
"Isn't She Pretty," is a beautiful Chromo, a splendid Parlor Picture, and a valuable work of art; it is highly finished, mounted and varnished, and *worth more than double the cost of subscription*, and together with DEMOREST'S MONTHLY affords an opportunity for the investment of Three Dollars *such as may never occur again*. Do not fail to subscribe for "DEMOREST'S MAGAZINE," and you will never be willing to be without it.
Address, **W. JENNINGS DEMOREST,**
838 Broadway, N. Y.
Specimen Copies of the Latest Nos. of the Magazine mailed free on receipt of 25 cents.

THOMSON'S NEW STYLES
GLOVE-FITTING CORSET.

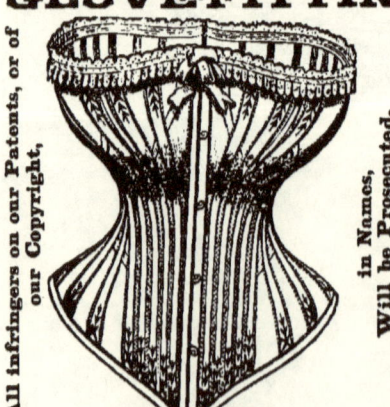

THE VENTILATING
OR
SUMMER CORSET
Entirely NEW in style and perfect in shape.
The **CURVILINEAR**, rich and elegant in finish.
Also, a lower cost
"GLOVE-FITTING,"
than ever before offered; which, with our former regular qualities, make the assortment complete.

These justly celebrated
**PATENT
GLOVE-FITTING CORSETS**
are constantly gaining favor in the United States, as well as in foreign countries.

All infringers on our Patents, or of our Copyright, in Names, Will be Prosecuted.

Always ask for **THOMSON'S Genuine Glove-Fitting Corsets**, every Corset being stamped with the name and Trade Mark, the Crown. For Sale by first class Dealers, Everywhere.
THOMSON, LANGDON & CO.,
Sole Patentees, 391 Broadway, N. Y.

WM. W. RIDER,
Linen Collars, Cuffs, Undersleeves,
SHIRTS AND SHIRT FRONTS,

Of Superior Quality, constantly on Hand, or made to order. A full assortment of the above goods, together with a Complete Stock of

Ladies' and Gents' Furnishing Goods,
AT
NO. 84 HUDSON STREET,
TWO DOORS WEST OF SOUTH PEARL.

POPULAR SHIRT AND COLLAR LAUNDRY.

Collars and Cuffs Laundried with Domestic Finish.

TRIMBLE OPERA HOUSE,
No. 31 South Pearl Street, Albany, N. Y.
ACADEMY OF MUSIC RE-BUILT.

LUCIEN BARNES, Manager.

WHEN YOU VISIT ALBANY
GO TO SEE

THE MOST BEAUTIFUL THEATRE IN THE WORLD.

The Most Beautiful Drop Curtain in America.

THE FINEST SCENERY OUT OF NEW YORK.

THE BEST ORCHESTRA EVER OUT OF NEW YORK.

The Best Company in the Country.

The only First Class Theatre in the State of New York out of the City of New York.

THE BEST STARS APPEAR FROM TIME TO TIME,

Giving to its Patrons a varied entertainment, and everything done in a FIRST CLASS STYLE.

SPECIAL FEATURE—
MATINEES!
WEDNESDAYS AND SATURDAYS.

VISIT
THE TWEDDLE HALL
DOLLAR STORE,
83 STATE ST.,
ALBANY, N. Y.

THE WAKEFIELD
Earth Closet,
Is by all odds the *best* yet patented. Send to Wakefield Earth Closet Co., 36 Dey St., New York, for Descriptive pamphlet, or call and examine.

CHINA TEA COMPANY,
Wholesale and Retail Dealers in
Teas, Coffees, Spices, &c.
137 MAIN STREET, ROCHESTER, N. Y.

W. H. BRUCE,
Bathing, Shaving and Hair Dressing Saloon,
Nine Chairs in constant Operation,
Masonic Block, cor. Buffalo and Exchange Streets, Rochester.

DR. ROBT. HAMILTON'S
MEDICAL INSTITUTE.
Opposite Congress Spring Park, Saratoga Springs, N. Y. Hot, Cold, Medicated Electro-Chemical Baths, Oxygenated Air, Sweedish Movement, and the Health Lift used in the treatment of FEMALE, LUNG, AND CHRONIC DISEASES. Send for a Circular, giving an account of its advantages, Certificates, Remarkable Cures, Testimonials, References, &c. During the Summer season the House is open to the public, and affords *FIRST CLASS ACCOMMODATIONS* at Reasonable Rates.

EXCELSIOR SPRING, SARATOGA SPRINGS. N. Y.
A. R. LAWRENCE & Co., Proprietors.
From Fordyce Barker, M. D., of New York, Professor of Obstetrics and Diseases of Women in the Bellevue Hospital Medical College.

I make great use of the various mineral waters in my practice, and I regard the "Excelsior" Spring Water of Saratoga as the best saline and alkaline laxative of this class. Sparkling with Carbonic Acid Gas, it is to most persons very agreeable to the taste, and prompt in action as a gentle diuretic and cathartic.   FORDYCE BARKER, M. D.

SARATOGA WATER CURE,
AND HYGIENIC INSTITUTION.
Located on Broadway, opposite Congress and Park Springs.

N. & B. T. BEDORTHA, M. D., Physicians and Surgeons.

Special Attention given to the use of the various Mineral Waters. Baths of all kinds, such as Hot, Cold, Spray, Sulphur Vapor, &c., &c.
For Circular, address
N. & B. T. BEDORTHA, M. D., Saratoga Springs, N. Y.

DR. FELIX GOURAUD'S
ORIENTAL CREAM or MAGICAL BEAUTIFIER.

This preparation has acquired a reputation which makes it sought after by ladies coming from or going to the most distant countries, for it has no equal or rival in its beautifying qualities. In removing Tan, Freckles, Sallowness, Moth, Patches, &c., its effects are almost magical. Like all other of Dr. Gouraud's preparations, this has extended its sale until it has become a specialty by its own merits, and is not the creature of mere advertising notoriety. It is recommended from one customer to another on actual knowledge of its value and utility. Prepared by Dr. Felix Gouraud, 48 Bond street (removed from 433 Broadway), New York, and to be had of all Druggists. Established 31 years.

Gouraud's Italian Medicated Soap cures Moth, Patches, Pimples, Freckles, Sallowness, Red Nose, Erysipelas, and all skin deformities. Established 31 years. Depot 48 Bond street, New York. Laboratory 55 Great Jones street.

☞ Beware of Lotions for the Skin containing mineral astringents utterly ruinous to the complexion, and by their repellant action positively injurious to health, frequently taking off the skin.

MRS. CASTLE'S
EMPORIUM OF FASHIONS.
DRESS AND CLOAK MAKING IN THE LATEST
Styles and on Short Notice.

A Perfect Fit Warranted. Call and see our Patterns.

MRS. CASTLE,
670 BROADWAY, ALBANY, N. Y.

S. T. Taylor's admirable System Taught. Also, Mrs. Leake's Diagram, two of the best Systems in use. Ladies are invited to test them. Satisfaction given or money refunded. Cutting, in all its branches, done at moderate prices, and satisfaction warranted in every case.

H. N. GARDNER,
Wholesale Dealer in
TANGER SOUND & BAY OYSTERS,
Fruits, Nuts, Figs, &c.,
666 Broadway, Albany, N. Y.
Clam in the Shell, by the barrel or 1000. Oranges and Lemons by the box, &c.

A. ARMBRUST,
MERCHANT TAILOR.
Clothing made to order in the neatest and best manner, and in the latest styles.

5 Clinton Avenue, Albany, N. Y.

E. A. HOBBS & CO.,
FAMILY GROCERIES,
Foreign and Domestic Fruits, Havana Cigars, Hermetically Sealed Goods, etc.

No. 7 Clinton Avenue, Albany, N. Y.

GARDNER,
(From Troy,)
Custom Manufacturer of the Celebrated
Perfect Fitting Dress Shirts.
Collars, Cuffs and Furnishing Goods at low Prices.
510 Broadway, Albany, N. Y.

G. W. GUTHINGER,
Dealer in
Furniture, & Upholsterer,
690 BROADWAY.
Window Shades, Mattresses, Pillows, Bolsters, &c.

S. E. MILLER,
Fashionable Hatter,
654 BROADWAY,
ALBANY, N. Y.

IRVING HOUSE,
MAIN STREET, CATSKILL, N. Y.
H. A. PERSON, Proprietor.

New Brick House, and New Furniture Throughout. Carriages and Omnibus to the Boats and Cars. Terms Reasonable.

STAGES FOR ALL POINTS WEST.

WORTH HOUSE, HUDSON, N. Y.

Centrally Located. Terms moderate.

CHAS. B. MILLER, Proprietor.

NOS. 81, 83, 85 WARREN STREET.

Albany Paper Collar Company,

MANUFACTURERS OF ALL STYLES

PAPER COLLARS and CUFFS.

SPECIALTY,

CLOTH COVERED COLLARS.

619 BROADWAY, ALBANY, N. Y.

DELAVAN HOUSE,

ALBANY,

CLARENDON HOTEL,

SARATOGA SPRINGS,

CHAS. E. LELAND,

PROPRIETOR.

NEW YORK AND TROY STEAMBOAT CO.
EVENING LINE DIRECT FROM
TROY AND ALBANY to NEW YORK.

VANDERBILT,
Capt. F. TESON, Commanding.

CONNECTICUT,
Capt. L. D. DEMING, Commanding.

Leave TROY every Evening for New York (except Saturdays) at 6 o'clock, stopping at ALBANY until the arrival of the Evening Cars from Saratoga Springs and the North.

THE STEAMER GOLDEN GATE,

Belonging to this Company, leaves Troy every Evening at 7 o'clock (except Saturdays and Sundays), to convey passengers for the above steamers down to them at Albany, Free of Charge.

☞ *Hudson River Railroad Tickets received, and Passage with State Room allowed for each of them.*

Freight handled with care, and Forwarded with Express Despatch.

RUSSELL P. CLAPP, Sup't., Troy, N. Y.

THE HUDSON RIVER BY DAYLIGHT,
THE DAY LINE OF STEAMBOATS
C. VIBBARD AND DANIEL DREW,

Leave New York, foot of Vestry St. at 8.30 A. M.,
And 34th St. at 8.45 A. M., daily, (Sundays excepted,)
Landing at Yonkers, (Tarrytown and Nyack by Ferry Boat,) Cozzens, West Point, Cornwall, Newburgh, Poughkeepsie, Rhinebeck, Catskill and Hudson, reaching Albany at 6 P. M.
Returning, leaves Albany from foot of Hamilton St. at 9 A. M., arriving at Albany at 6 P. M.

AFTERNOON BOAT FROM NEW YORK.
The favorite Steamboat
MARY POWELL,

For Newburgh, Poughkeepsie and Rondout, landing at Cozzens, West Point, Cornwall and Milton, leaves New York from Vestry Street Pier at 3½ o'clock P. M. Returning, leaves Rondout at 5.30 A. M., arriving at New York at 11 A. M.

ISAAC L. WELSH, G. T. A.

LETTER FROM NEW YORK.

There are thousands of "Letters" written from the Metropolis every year, yet the story of its shows and pleasures, its charities and business enterprises, is never exhausted. The rogue and the upright man of business jostle each other in the streets, while the "Divorce-without-publicity" lawyer, rooms in the same building with the city missionary, and the reports of the press are only incomplete attempts to winnow the chaff from the wheat. There are thousands of business enterprises in New York conducted by men of honor and sagacity, whose business might be ten times quadrupled if it were known throughout the country that they can guarantee remunerative employment to an immense number of worthy and energetic persons.

We have faith to believe that practical benevolence will yet devise some labor exchange upon a gigantic scale, by which the "laborers who stand idle" may be directed to the work which will yield them the most ready and sure returns.

These were our thoughts as we recently visited the warerooms of the

Eugenic Manufacturing Company,

At 142 FULTON STREET, NEW YORK CITY.

We believe there are branch establishments in other parts of the city; but this office, with its unpretending engraved sign, is the centre of the company's large wholesale and retail trade.

Entering, we are shown into a Ladies' Reception Room, and find ourselves attended by a pleasant lady, who exhibits articles which are required in every household, and yet which cannot generally be purchased at the stores. Several factories are running constantly to supply the goods for this firm. Many of the goods are patented by the Eugenic Manufacturing Co., and can be obtained only of them. Numerous other articles may perhaps be obtained elsewhere, but the assortment is larger and the prices are lower here, on account of their facilities for manufacturing. LADIES' DRESS SHIELDS, CHILDREN'S BIBS of pure and perfumed rubber, and of various sizes, are kept here. Rubber Gloves, the value of which to those who wish to protect their hands while engaged in household duties, which naturally "leave their mark," can scarcely be estimated. Skirt supporters, Bay State Corsets, the best in the market, and also every device for convenience and comfort in which rubber plays a part. We cannot possibly enumerate here, but would say to those interested who live at a distance, "send for a circular." Ladies who seek profitable employment cannot do better than to take an agency for the sale of such goods. There is no risk, and the profits are very fair. They are articles which are needed everywhere. Many a person who keeps a small fancy store might largely increase the profits of business by adding these goods to their stock. For terms, etc., apply to the Company, 142 Fulton Street, New York. We will only say in conclusion, that this firm is eminently reliable. They may be trusted to deal honorably in every particular with their agents.

As the Season opens, there are many who may find it profitable to canvass in the villages and towns of this State, who would perhaps scarcely care, from a feeling of pride, to engage in the same business in the cities in which they reside. We trust that these brief suggestions may be of benefit to some who desire "Paying Employment." Our "letter" has been written with a view to their benefit alone, by a Lady who has been much benefitted by the productions of the Eugenic Manufacturing Company, and one who aims to befriend her sex.

A FRIEND.

TIME TESTS THE MERITS OF ALL THINGS.

1840——TO——1871.

For Thirty-One Years
PERRY DAVIS'S
PAIN KILLER

Has been tested in every variety of climate, and by almost every nation known to Americans. It is the almost constant companion and inestimable friend of the missionary and the traveler, on sea and land, and no one should travel on our LAKES OR RIVERS WITHOUT IT.

Pain Killer was the First, and is the Only Permanent Pain Reliever.

Since the PAIN KILLER was first introduced, and met with such unsurpassed sale, many, LINIMENTS, RELIEFS, PANACEAS and other REMEDIES have been offered to the public, but not one of them has ever attained the truly ENVIABLE STANDING of the PAIN KILLER.

WHY IS THIS SO?

It is because DAVIS'S PAIN KILLER is what it claimed to be, a Reliever of Pain. Its merits are unsurpassed.

If you are suffering from INTERNAL PAIN, *Twenty or Thirty Drops in a Little Water* will almost instantly cure you. There is nothing to equal it. In a few moments it cures Colic, Cramps, Spasms, Heartburn, Diarrhœa, Dysentary, Flux, Wind in the Bowels, Sour Stomach, Dyspepsia, Sick Headache. In sections of the country where

FEVER AND AGUE

Prevails, there is no remedy held in greater esteem. Persons traveling should keep it by them. A few drops, in water, will prevent sickness or bowel troubles from change of water.

From foreign countries the calls for PAIN KILLER are great. It is found to cure CHOLERA, when all other remedies fail. When used externally, as a Liniment, nothing gives quicker ease in *Burns, Cuts, Bruises, Sprains, Stings from Insects, and Scalds.* It removes the fire, and the wound heals like ordinary sores. Those suffering with Rheumatism, Gout, or Neuralgia, if not a positive cure, they find the PAIN KILLER gives them relief when no other remedy will. It gives

Instant Relief from Aching Teeth.

From 1840 to this day, 1871, (Thirty-one Years,) PERRY DAVIS'S PAIN KILLER has had no rival.

Every housekeeper should keep it at hand, to apply it on the first attack of any Pain. It will give satisfactory relief, and save hours of suffering.

Do not trifle with yourselves by trusting untried remedies. Be sure you call for, and get the genuine PAIN KILLER, as many worthless nostrums are attempted to be sold on the great reputation of this valuable medicine. Directions accompany each bottle.

Price 25 Cents, 50 Cents, and $1.00 per Bottle.

CAMILLE PERFUME
FOR THE
HANDKERCHIEF,
Sold by all Druggists.

PREPARED ONLY BY

CHARLES M. MORRIS,
PERFUMER,
6 NORTON STREET,
ALBANY, N. Y.

One application warranted to retain its fragrance one week.

Use it and convince yourselves.

Samples furnished to Dealers, if desired, before purchasing.

PYLE'S O. K. SOAP,
SALERATUS
AND
CREAM TARTAR,
A FIRST CLASS ARTICLE,

Designed for the best Family Trade,

AND WILL SPEAK FOR THEMSELVES ON TRIAL.

Sold by First Class Grocers Everywhere.

JAMES PYLE, Manufacturer,
350 WASHINGTON STREET,
NEW YORK.

FIRST PREMIUM COOK STOVE.

THE IMPROVED
NEW EMPIRE
COOKING STOVE.

Awarded the First Premium at the New York State Fair, 1870.

Manufactured by SWETT, QUIMBY & PERRY,

No. 277 River Street, TROY, N. Y.

THE BEST COLORING EXTANT
FOR THE HAIR,

AND THE EASIEST APPLIED, IS

BOSWELL & WARNER'S
COLORIFIC.

It Colors the **Hair** to a **Beautiful Brown** or **Black** by merely moistening the Hair with the **Colorific.**

It does not Crisp or Burn the Hair, but renders it Smooth and Glossy without any other Preparation.

It contains no Lead or Sulphur, or any article the least injurious.

For Sale by all PATENT MEDICINE DEALERS and DRUGGISTS generally.

H. C. BOSWELL, Proprietor,

155 Grand Street, Williamsburgh, N. Y.

Depot in the City of New York, 9 Dey Street.

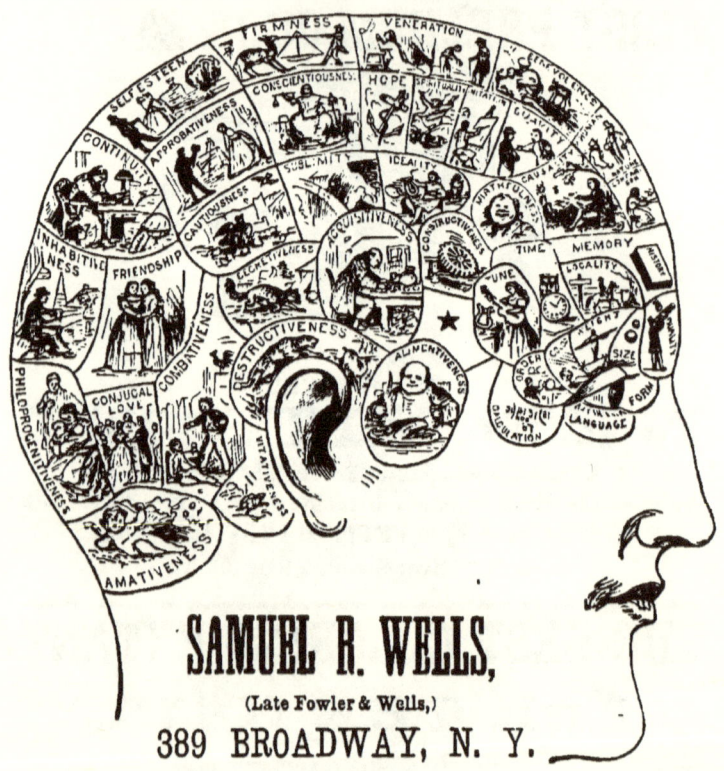

SAMUEL R. WELLS,
(Late Fowler & Wells,)
389 BROADWAY, N. Y.

Among the many places of interest in NEW YORK city, strangers and others should not overlook THE PHRENOLOGICAL MUSEUM at 389 Broadway. Here are many things to interest and instruct. Especially would we call attention to the fine collection of casts. Here we have busts (not models) of the most noted of good and bad men—among them casts of Aaron Burr, Horace Mann, William Cullen Bryant, Horace Greeley, Napoleon the First, Laura Bridgman, and a long list of others far too numerous to mention here. There is also a large collection of human and animal *crania* with an innumerable number of pictures and portraits. The rooms are always open and free. Mr. S. R. WELLS, the present proprietor, is also Editor and Publisher of the PHRENOLOGICAL JOURNAL, a Magazine of undoubted excellence, and Publisher of a large list of useful and practical Books.

NARRAGANSETT STEAMSHIP CO.,

FOR BOSTON
Via Newport and Fall River.

1871.   1871.

DAILY, (Sundays included,) AT

5 P. M. from Pier 30, North River.

FOOT OF CHAMBERS ST.

The Magnificent Steamers

BRISTOL
COMMANDER A. G. SIMMONS,

—AND—

PROVIDENCE
COMMANDER B. M. SIMMONS.

The Most Direct Route to Taunton, Middleboro, Plymouth, New Bedford, Martha's Vineyard, Nantucket, the South Shore of Massachusetts, and all points on the Cape Cod Railway.

GRAND PROMENADE CONCERT

On Board each Steamer every Evening,
By HALL'S Celebrated Boston Brass, String and Reed Bands.
For Tickets or State Rooms apply at

241 Broadway; 529 Broadway, corner of Spring Street; Broadway, corner 23d Street; No. 4 Court Street, Brooklyn, or at the Office on the Pier.

Freight Received up to 5 o'oclock P. M.

M. R. SIMONS, Managing Director.   JAMES FISK, JR., President.
H. H. MANGAM, Gen'l Freight Ag't.   CHAS. B. KIMBALL, Gen'l Pass. Ag't.

WILL ALL THOSE WHO SUFFER
FROM
CONSUMPTION OR COUGH,
PLEASE
READ THE FOLLOWING LETTER,
FROM A RELIABLE DRUGGIST?

MOUNT VERNON, ILL., April 29, 1871.

Messrs. J. N. HARRIS & Co., Cincinnati, Ohio:

Gentlemen,—I heard one of my customers speak in such high terms of Allen's Lung Balsam to-day, that I thought I would write you the substance of his statement. He says his mother, who is now sixty years of age, has suffered with consumption for several years, and has been under the care of all our best physicians, but never received any permanent benefit; then she resorted to most every kind of Cough and Lung Balsam that could be procured for her, but all to no avail. She still grew worse, until she was confined to her bed; and when she was seized with a paroxysm of coughing she would lose the power of respiration, and they were compelled to resort to various means to restore breathing; and while she coughed so hard she could not expectorate anything, and the family and friends had given up all hopes of her recovery. Her son noticed the advertisement of Allen's Lung Balsam in the Christian Advocate, and they thought they would procure and try it. They commenced giving her the Balsam at 5 o'clock p. m., as directed, a dose every hour until midnight; then she took another spell of coughing, and expectorated a mouth full of dark yellow matter, which was something she had not been able to do for some time. They continued to give her the Balsam until morning, and then she began to expectorate freely, and within two hours she had expectorated three pints of mucus matter, which gave her immediate relief, and since that time she has continued to improve. She now sits up all day, and can walk about the house and take considerable out-door exercise. Her son bought more of the Balsam to-day, and he is recommending it very highly to every one.

Yours, respectfully, A. C. JOHNSON, Druggist.

Was there ever greater proof of merit than the case this letter refers to?

ALLEN'S LUNG BALSAM

Is without doubt the Best Expectorant Remedy ever offered to the afflicted public. It contains no opium in any form, and its use is harmless to the most delicate.

☞ Directions accompany each bottle.

ALLEN'S LUNG BALSAM

Has proved itself to be the greatest medical remedy for healing the lungs, purifying the blood, and restoring the tone of the liver. It excites the phlegm which is raised from the lungs, thereby the cough, pains, oppression, night sweats, and difficulty of breathing, all the above symptoms will be cured, and the whole system again restored to health.

For Sale by all Medicine Dealers.

A·A·Constantine's
PERSIAN HEALING, OR PINE TAR SOAP.

Each cake is stamped "A. A. Constantine's Persian Healing, or Pine Tar Soap. Patented March 12th, 1867." No other genuine.

FOR THE TOILET, BATH AND NURSERY,

This Soap has no equal. It makes the complexion fair, preserves the skin soft and healthy, removes all dandruff, keeps the hair soft and silky, and prevents it from falling off, and is "the best **Hair Renovator** in use."

It cures Chapped Hands, Pimples, Salt Rheum, Frosted Feet, Burns, all Diseases of the Scalp and Skin, Catarrh of the Head, and is

A GOOD SHAVING SOAP.

BALDNESS CURED.

I can recommend your Persian Healing Soap for Baldness; it is bringing my hair in beautifully. I consider it the best Hair Renovator.

M. H. COMBS, 218 Atlantic Street, Brooklyn, N. Y.

The wife of the Rev. N. Brown, twenty years a Missionary in Southern Asia, writes from Jersey City, N. J., to A. A. Constantine: We have been using your soap in our family for toilet purposes, and find its healing and cleansing qualities so far exceed our expectations, or anything of the kind we have ever used before, that we cannot do without it. Indeed, we find it the household remedy for almost everything. If we get a bruise, cut, or burn, the resort is immediately to the Constantine Soap, and in some cases the cures have been wonderful.

I recommended it to a friend who had a very annoying annual eruption on the skin; he used it a short time, and was cured. I have recommended it to others, who have used it, and always with success. From actual knowledge, I consider it a great curative in cutaneous eruptions. I have used it for catarrh in the head, making a suds, and snuffing it through the nose, and it has cured me. I use it constantly for the TOILET, and consider it the BEST SOAP FOR THAT PURPOSE.

R. BENSON, U. S. Life Ins, Co., 48 Wall St., N. Y.

I have used your Persian Healing Soap in my practice, extensively, and it has proved the best healing soap I ever used. It has no equal as a soap for washing the heads and skin of children.

L. P. ALDRICH, M. D., 19 Harrison St., N. Y.

We have given it a full and fair trial. In the bath-room and nursery, and also as an excellent shaving Soap, we think it is unsurpassed. We recommend it honestly.—*Methodist Home Journal.*

This Soap has already won the praise and esteem of very many of our first families in New York and throughout the country.

It is used extensively by our best Physicians. Wherever used it has become

A HOUSEHOLD NECESSITY,

We advise all to try it. For sale by all Dealers. Agents wanted. Call on or address

A. A. CONSTANTINE & CO.
43 ANN STREET, NEW YORK.

J. MUNSELL,

STEAM

PRINTING HOUSE,

No. 82 STATE STREET,

ALBANY, N. Y.,

GIVES SPECIAL ATTENTION TO

TOWN AND COUNTY HISTORIES

GENEALOGIES, &c.,

As well as to every other kind of

BOOKS, PERIODICALS,

AND

PAMPHLETS.

By recent additions of New fonts of Book Type of the most approved faces, for Letter Press or Stereotype Printing, and the use of the latest improvements in presses, moved by steam, he is enabled, by the assistance of skillful workmen, to execute every description of orders in superior style, and with satisfactory promptness.

PUBLISHES

ANNALS OF ALBANY.

10 Vols. 12 mo., Cloth, Illustrated, $20.

HENRY C. HASKELL,
Albany Iron and Machine Works,

Nos. 50, 52, 54, and 56 Liberty, and 8 Pruyn Street,
OFFICE 8 PRUYN ST., NEAR STEAMBOAT LANDING,
ALBANY, NEW YORK.

Successor to PRUYN & LANSING in this branch of Business,

MANUFACTURER OF ALL SIZES OF

STEAM ENGINES AND BOILERS,

Bridge and Roof Bolts, Cemetery, Area and Stoop Railings, Bank Counter, Office and Desk Railings,

IRON WORK OF ALL KINDS,

Balconies, Verandas, Iron Bridges, Bedsteads, Bank Vaults, Wrought Iron Beams, Roof Crestings, Doors and Shutters.

MANUFACTURERS, ALSO, OF

REYNER, STONE & CO.'S

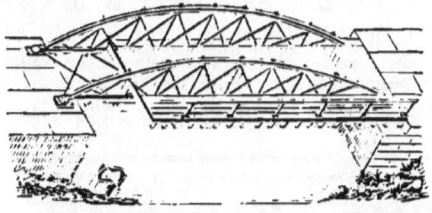

PATENT IMPROVED
WROUGHT-IRON TUBULAR ARCH TRUSS BRIDGE.

A Lithograph giving full particulars will be sent on application.

Particular Attention Given to Repairing all kinds of Machinery and Boilers.
PATTERNS AND MODELS MADE AT SHORT NOTICE.
SEND FOR ILLUSTRATED CATALOGUE.

POLLAK & SON,

MANUFACTURERS OF MEERSCHAUM PIPES,

AND DEALERS IN SEGARS.

Wholesale — 43 MAIDEN LANE, NEW YORK.

Retail — 27 JOHN STREET. In the Middle of the Block.

WIDOWS' AND ORPHANS' BENEFIT LIFE INSURANCE CO.,

OFFICE, No. 132 BROADWAY, N. Y.
ASSETS OVER $1,500,000.

CHARLES H. RAYMOND, Pres't.   G. S. WINSTON, M. D., Med. Exam'r.
ROBERT A. GRANNIS, Secretary.   SHEPPARD HOMANS, Cons'g Act'y.
WM. BETTS, LL.D., Counsel.

Issues all approved forms of Life and Endowment Policies. The attention of careful business men is invited to the RESERVE DIVIDEND PLAN, as adopted by this Company, and which is original with it. Full information may be obtained by application to the Company's Office.

FRANK CHAMBERLAIN, Gen'l Manager for N. Y. State, 449 Broadway, Albany.

AGENTS WANTED,
FOR
THE YEAR OF BATTLES,

A History of the War Between France and Germany,

By L. P. BROCKETT, M. D.

This is the only complete work on the War published. Besides being an accurate History of the War, it embraces, also, an historical account of the Civil War in France, closing with the subversion of the Commune.

25,000 Have Been Sold in 60 days. The Most Remarkable Book Success of the Year.

Any live man or woman can sell 25 every day. Send $1.25 for outfit at once, or address,   H. S. GOODSPEED & CO.,
37 Park Row, New York.

IMPORTANT TO LADIES!
THE "EUGENIE,"
OR LADY'S COMPANION,
Patented November 17, 1868,

is a Periodical Bandage, recommended by many eminent Physicians, commended by nearly every Lady at sight, and is destined to be worn by every Young Miss and Married or Single Lady, of whatever position in life.

Price, $2; profits liberal, and sells readily. Agents wanted everywhere.
For Descriptive Circular, etc., address

THE "EUGENIE" MANUFACTURING CO.,
P. O. Box 2138.   142 *Fulton Street*, N. Y.

Ladies are invited to call and examine. A Lady always in attendance.

www.ingramcontent.com/pod-product-compliance
Lightning Source LLC
Chambersburg PA
CBHW030010240426
43672CB00007B/897